The Prophet:
Friend of God

The Prophet: Friend of God

Ed Dufresne

Ed Dufresne Ministries
Temecula, California

Unless otherwise indicated,
all scriptural quotations are taken from
the *King James Version* of the Bible.

The Prophet Friend of God
ISBN 0-940763-05-2
Copyright © 1989 by
Ed Dufresne Ministries
P.O. Box 186
Temecula, CA 92593
U.S.A.

Published by
Ed Dufresne Publications
P.O. Box 186
Temecula, CA 92593
U.S.A.

Printed in the United States of America.
All rights reserved under International
Copyright Law. Contents and/or cover may
not be reproduced in whole or in part in any
form without the express written consent of
the publisher.

Contents

Foreword

1. Characteristics of a True Prophet   1

2. "I Ordained Thee a Prophet"   19

3. Different Ranks and Different Anointings   41

4. Glimpses Into the Future   59

Books by Ed Dufresne

Devil, Don't Touch My Stuff

There's A Healer In The House

Fresh Oil From Heaven

Praying God's Word

The Prophet: Friend of God

Chapter 1
Characteristics of a True Prophet

There is so much misunderstanding about the prophet's ministry, or office, that I want to examine it in this book. Also the Lord has released me to do more teaching on the prophet's ministry because of things that will be happening in that ministry in the 1990s.

I want to obey God to the fullest so the Body of Christ will not be ignorant concerning the prophet's ministry, and so those who have the prophet's mantle will be helped to flow into their ministry.

When we preachers taught on the fivefold ministry gifts in the past, we touched on them lightly, saying, "Well, these are the types of ministry gifts, and this is how they operate. . . ." That was adequate then, but now a greater depth of understanding, more light and illumination, is coming — especially on the prophet's ministry.

During the next two years, which are crucial, the prophets must get before God and listen to what the Spirit of God is saying in this hour. *The prophets must speak by the inspiration of the Holy Ghost!*

The Lord spoke this to my heart: *"Revival won't come to America until the prophets get up and speak and prophesy."*

Teaching alone isn't going to get it. Pastoring alone isn't going to get it. Holding evangelistic meetings alone isn't going to get it. Unless the prophets come forth and speak, our country is in trouble.

America needs prophets who can't be bought with a

The Prophet: Friend of God

price . . . prophets who won't "pimp" their ministries for a price . . . prophets who will obey God . . . prophets who will go to any church God leads them, whether big or small.

We need the prophet's ministry to emerge in the forefront.

We need to hear what the Spirit of God is saying.

We need the prophets in this land to speak so we can have revival!

Yet, I've never seen such disrespect toward God and his prophets. Some ministers get cocky. They think they know everything about all the ministry gifts.

I used to come out of meetings and complain to the Lord, "I'm never going back to that church again! What's wrong with those harebrained people?"

Then the Lord answered, "Son, you've got to teach them about the office of the prophet — and don't call my people harebrained!"

How many churches really teach on the prophet's ministry? Most Pentecostal denominations know nothing about the prophet's ministry, and many Full Gospel churches know little about the prophet's ministry!

Someone told me that the pastor of a Full Gospel church said, "Well, God doesn't use prophets today. The prophet's ministry has been done away with." This was a *Full Gospel* church!

People seem to think a prophet (or prophetess) is someone like John the Baptist: a weirdo who lives in a remote place, eats strange things, has long hair, and hasn't taken a bath in thirty years.

On the other hand, another problem today is that many people are going around saying, "I'm a prophet." Watch out for anyone who says, "I'm this and I'm that" all the time!

Characteristics of a True Prophet

Proverbs 18:16 says that your gift will make room for you. *The Body of Christ will recognize the prophet's anointing on you.* You won't need to tell everyone, "I'm a prophet, and you must listen to me!"

(And just because you operate the simple *gift* of prophecy occasionally and prophesy does not make you a prophet. It does not mean that God has ordained you into the *office* of prophet.)

Prophets and apostles are now coming on the scene, as we will see in the last chapter of this book. But for now, we need to look at the nine major characteristics of a true prophet of God.

A Characteristic of Revelation

The first characteristic of a true *prophet* is that he is a man of revelation.

Evangelists and *pastors* are concerned especially with the people. If an evangelist is not concerned about people, he is not a true evangelist. And if a pastor is not concerned about people, he's not a true shepherd.

Many people, including singers who travel around, are called "evangelists," but they are really *exhorters*, even though souls are born again under their ministries. Such singers, musicians, psalmists, and others in the ministry of helps are set in the Church, but they are not evangelists. An evangelist is one who has miracles, signs, and wonders following his ministry.

Teachers are concerned with the Scriptures. They are very important to the Body of Christ; however, if they are not careful, they can lead the Body in the wrong direction. We need to pray that the teachers will teach accurately.

Apostles are men send from God with a special message — sent ones who go — special ones anointed to do special things.

The Prophet: Friend of God

A Characteristic of Knowledge

Resident in the prophet is the counsel of God. He has the heart and the pulse of God. Therefore, he can distinguish between the true and the false. This is the second characteristic of a true prophet.

It's important for the prophet to speak and bring revelation to the Church. How else can the teachers teach anything unless the prophets prophesy? When a true prophet prophesies, revelation comes. Then the teachers who were set in the Church can build on that foundation by teaching believers about things that are to come and things that need to be corrected.

Characteristics of False Prophets

Jeremiah 23:16-18 says:

> **Thus saith the Lord of hosts, Hearken not unto the words of the prophets that prophesy unto you: they make you vain: they speak a vision of their own heart, and not out of the mouth of the Lord.**
>
> **They say still unto them that despise me, The Lord hath said, Ye shall have peace; and they say unto every one that walketh after the imagination of his own heart, No evil shall come upon you.**
>
> **For who hath stood in the counsel of the Lord, and hath perceived and heard his word? who hath marked his word, and heard it?**

A *true* prophet will spend time in prayer, hear the voice of the Lord, get the counsel of God, and then go out and deliver it — whether it's popular or not!

A *false* prophet will put vanity in you by puffing you up all the time. You see, there's a difference between exhortation and encouragement from a true prophet and puffing people up from "a hireling prophet."

There are a lot of Holy Ghost "nightclubs" and "bless-me clubs" around, where people prophesy over each other, saying, "Well, this one's a prophet and that one's a prophet." They're not. These false prophets are just full of hot air.

Watch out for the person who butters you up all the time, saying things like, "Oh, you're great." Nobody is great but the Lord Jesus Christ!

What else is Jeremiah saying in the passage we just read? Verse 17 tells us that false prophets prophesy out of their imagination: *They imagine things.*

Verse 18, on the other hand, says that true prophets are habitually before God, hearing the counsel of God, so they speak out of what they have heard.

God has been dealing with me that I must spend more time with Him; I can't minister and take care of the business office and everything else. God sent me good people to do that so I can seek counsel from Him.

People frequently phone me and ask, "Have you got a *word* for me?"

"Yes, I've got a *word* for you — go read the Word."

A true prophet can't turn the gift on anytime he wants to! That's not how it works. That mantle must come on you to prophesy. It's exercised *as the Spirit wills.*

I travel all over the country. Pastors often recognize me in meetings and say, "Well, come on up here, Ed. You've got something." I may have an *inkling* of something, and perhaps I could get up and *predict* some things out of my own spirit, but they try to force me.

"No, no. You've got something," they insist. "Come up and prophesy."

I can't get up and just prophesy at will! Some people do get up and say, "Thus saith the Lord. . . ." They're so eloquent; it's just like they're reading their prophecy. But I can't do that. The anointing must come upon me before I can prophesy.

The Prophet: Friend of God

A Characteristic of Friendship

It says in Amos 3:7 and Exodus 33:11 that *prophets are friends of God.* That's the third important characteristic of a true prophet. I like that.

> **Surely the Lord God will do nothing but he revealeth his secret unto his servants the prophets.**
>
> **Amos 3:7**

> **And the Lord spake unto Moses face to face, as a man speaketh unto his friend. . . .**
>
> **Exodus 33:11**

Another man who was a friend of God and who walked with Him was the prophet Enoch:

> **And Enoch walked with God: and he was not; for God took him.**
>
> **Genesis 5:24**

Don't mess around with God's friends! As David pointed out, you must not touch a prophet of God:

> **Touch not mine anointed, and do my prophets no harm.**
>
> **Psalm 105:15**

David practiced this in his own life. Once when King Saul was in hot pursuit of David and his men, David had a perfect opportunity to kill Saul in a dark cave — but his respect for "the anointing of the Lord" that was on Saul restrained him. In the dramatic confrontation that followed, David said to his enemy Saul:

> **Behold, this day thine eyes have seen how that the Lord had delivered thee to day into mine hand in the cave; and some bade me kill thee; but mine eye spared thee; and I said, I will not put forth mine hand against my lord; for he is the Lord's anointed.**
>
> **1 Samuel 24:10**

Even if he's in error, don't touch God's anointed! "Well,

we're not like him." What do you mean, you're not *like* him? "Him" is part of you — a part of the Body of Christ — I don't care what he's done. Furthermore, love covers a multitude of sins (1 Peter 4:8).

A Characteristic of Demonstration

The fourth characteristic of the true prophet is that prophets or prophetesses are men and women of demonstrations. To reveal what God has given them, they often must act strangely, or literally *act out* or demonstrate their sermons.

To the carnal or natural mind, their actions seem odd in a religious setting. In fact, they may do things that will cause your intellect to say, "Oh my, how disgusting!" But *prophets are different.* You can't figure out a prophet of God, so don't knock what you don't understand.

For years, people used to call me "Wild Eddie." Then I tried to be a dignified teacher, but it nearly killed me, due to the fact that sometimes we prophets must demonstrate or physically display our message. I want you to know "Wild Eddie" is back — and I'm going to get wilder!

It's wise to carry a tape recorder around a prophet if you travel with him. You never know when he's going to go into the Spirit and prophesy, or even do something strange.

Often, God will have me do strange things in the prayer line, jerking people, laying my hands on their head and speaking in tongues, or whatever.

Another prophet and I once talked in tongues back and forth and I heard him in English, which is scriptural. (See Acts 2:6-11.)

And talk about *strange* — in a back room after a church service one night in Tulsa, the power of God hit me and I began spinning like a top in the Spirit.

Some people may think, "Oh, that couldn't be of God."

The Prophet: Friend of God

You should never say that, because you haven't seen anything yet. And spinning like that *is* in the Bible: God came down in a whirlwind and caught several people up to heaven. We're talking about some *strange* things! Read the Bible.

You can't figure God out. You're trying to figure Him out in your head, wondering, "Why this? Why that?" Just jump in.

"How do we *know* if it's of God?"

Well, whoever gets the glory after it's done ought to tell the story right there. You certainly aren't going to stand up and say, "Glory to the devil!" if it's of God.

Someone must teach about these things, because some of them are going to happen in this next revival, and we're all going to need to understand them.

Of course, the timing must be right for these teachings. Otherwise, people will get squirrelly. Someone will go out and think he's a prophet. (Maybe he prophesied once or had a vision or dream.) He'll get weird, grow a beard, live on the side of a mountain, and have five wives, or something like that.

Or else he'll go from church to church and announce he's been called by God to straighten churches out. So he'll sit in the back, and after the meeting, he'll start prophesying to everyone: "Thus saith the Lord: You married the wrong one. You need to divorce your husband and marry someone else." (And that's probably just what that whoremongering spirit wanted to hear in the first place!)

People cannot call themselves into the prophet's office. We're in danger right now in the Body of Christ because people who are not anointed are trying to walk in the prophet's office and other offices.

Make sure you stay in your own office. It's dangerous to try to walk in any office you're not anointed for! Intruding into the wrong office can kill you! And don't be taken up with names or titles. Just let God promote you in due season.

Many pastors should not be pastors, for they are actually businessmen. They may die prematurely. Why? Because they did not discern their part in the Body of Christ. They are not where they belong. They have lost their effectiveness for God. They will end up being shortchanged in life.

A Characteristic of Confrontation

Fifth, by nature, *prophets are men and women of confrontation.* It seems like they're always going a different way from the rest of the crowd. Furthermore, prophets confront people with their sins.

Nathan said to David, regarding his affair with Bathsheba, "Thou art the man." (That didn't make him very popular.)

Elijah made fun of the prophets of Baal before he slew them. (That made Jezebel decide to kill him.)

John the Baptist told Herod and his wife that they were living in sin. (That caused John to be beheaded.)

It doesn't make you popular when you go against the grain. I know what I'm talking about, because I've been in churches where the pastor's wife had a Jezebel spirit and wanted to run the church.

And if you don't bow down to a Jezebel like that, she'll try to get rid of you one way or another! As a matter of fact, I've been asked to leave some churches because the pastor's wife didn't like what I said, and because I didn't recognize the "anointing" she thought she had on her life.

If these Jezebels don't get their way, they have little "fits." I do not bow down to Jezebel spirits; I don't care whose church it is. (I'll get to the men a little later. I'm not picking on the ladies here.)

The Prophet: Friend of God

Confrontation With a Jezebel

After a conference in a hotel, a woman came after me in the restaurant. She started out, "I just want you to know, brother, that we *love* you." (Those were the "vain words." Look out!) "We love you and everything, *but*. . . ." (Watch out for those "buts.")

"You know, my husband got offended by the way you prayed for him tonight."

It just came up out of my spirit — I replied, "What was he doing in the line, then?"

"Well, you could have been more gentle about the way you put your hands on his head." (That's a religious devil speaking.)

I thought, "Why isn't her husband over here telling me about it? Why is *she* telling me these things?"

And the Lord said, "She's got a Jezebel spirit."

She continued, "Well, he didn't *really* want to go up there in the first place." (It turned out he was a minister in a large denomination that is opposed to the gifts of the Spirit in operation.)

And I said — just as nicely as I could — "Well, ma'am, he should never have gotten in the line."

She was dictating to God and me how God should minister to him! Now, if I need to be corrected, I am willing to be corrected. Prophets can get into error just like anyone else. (If they don't live right, prophets can get dingy, too, and think they're seeing visions when they're actually seeing devils — but they can't tell the difference.)

Never, never pray to be a prophet unless you can handle confrontations! And as the anointing gets stronger, the confrontations get heavier.

When God tells you to speak, you *must* say what God says. You're God's man or God's woman. You're God's friend. You hear God's voice. You get counsel from God.

Confrontation With Adultery

I was in a meeting once in the Midwest and all of a sudden God said, "This church is full of adultery." He said, "They're swapping wives."

I stood in front of the center section, and I asked two minister friends of mine who were present to stand in front of the side sections. I had everyone pray.

Those who were participating in this sin didn't come forward, so I said, "Now, Bob, you go and get that man over there. I'm going to get this one over here." My friend Mark looked at me, and I've never seen him pray so hard in my life! But he headed toward a man near the wall. God took him straight to the guilty man.

You talk about a confrontation and a demonstration by three men of God. Those men could have been set free from the bondage of that adulterous spirit, but they would not come forward and repent. The prophet's word to them was not of doom or gloom. If they had accepted it, it would have brought light into their lives.

But it didn't make me popular with the pastor. In fact, he never invited me back. The Lord was trying to help his church. The operation of the prophet's ministry brought light.

Ignoring the Prophets

Many have criticized the fall of the leaders of large ministries. Did you know there were several prophets who were sent to those organizations to prophesy? Many of the things that happened there would never have happened if the leaders had listened to the prophets — but they didn't.

Do you know why they didn't? Because they didn't discern the prophet's ministry that is in the Body of Christ.

The Prophet: Friend of God

What happened was, the message was aborted. The devil will always come in and try to abort the prophet's message.

One way he's currently doing it is through the teaching that goes, "I'm an apostle [or prophet] over your church. Let me in. Submit." No, there must first be a covenant relationship between the prophet and the congregation.

For example, there are people across the nation who say, "Brother Ed, we love you. We recognize you as a prophet. We've watched your ministry through the years, and we're telling you that you're a prophet to this church when you come and speak." That's not lifting me up. But for me to go to a church where there's no relationship or covenant like this and say, "Submit" would be hogwash.

Before I start a meeting in a church, I don't want the pastor to unload all his church problems on me. Pastors sometimes start doing this when they pick me up at the airport: "Well, we've got this problem and we've got that problem."

I'll say, "Shhh! Don't tell me anything, or I won't be able to help you." I can't do a thing for them myself; the Spirit of God must be in manifestation. I need to minister to the whole church prophetically, through the gifts of the Spirit.

In situations like this, a prophet will speak right out of his spirit and prophesy. That's why it's difficult for me to preach or teach using notes: I'll start preaching in another direction, saying things by the unction of the Spirit.

I'll go into a meeting praying, "Lord, just let me be a *sweet teacher* — everyone loves a sweet teacher." I'll try to preach on healing, but God will mess up my notes. He won't let me preach on healing; He'll want me to talk about someone living in adultery! That's confrontation, and we're going to see more of it in the future. That's why I'm teaching about it.

That's why you need to discern these parts that God

set in the Church. Pastors, that's why it's good to have the different gift ministries come into your church.

True prophecy will enrich and enhance our relationship with the Lord and with each other. It will make us more dependent on the Lord. It will not lead to an unhealthy dependence on the prophet.

Private Confrontations

God has said to me, "Yes, I speak through the prophets. The prophets are going to be saying some things to kings and heads of countries by the Spirit." Look at Proverbs 21:1. "The king's heart is in the hand of the Lord . . . he turneth it whithersoever he will."

Why will this happen? As we read in Amos 3:7, "Surely the Lord God will do nothing but he revealeth his secret unto his servants the prophets."

God will reveal secret things to His prophets, and the prophets will have to obey what God said. However, this does not mean they have to do it *publicly.* As a matter of fact, some prophets haven't been saying things publicly these days; what they've been saying has been mostly behind closed doors.

Many people think a prophet *must* get up in front of a crowd in order to prophesy, but he can prophesy in his prayer time, or in a private gathering and change things and deal with things in the spirit realm *as that anointing or mantle comes upon him.*

A prime example of a man with the rank of "general" in the prophet's ministry today is Kenneth E. Hagin. Although Brother Hagin is a teacher of the Word of God, he also stands in the office of prophet. He's one of the prophets whom God is using in these last days, and he's in what we'd call the last phase of his ministry.

I use him as a prime example of the prophet's ministry because he's been my teacher; I've sat under his ministry.

The Prophet: Friend of God

And he's the principal prophet who has imparted things from his mantle to me through the years. I've watched his humility and meekness. He's been in the ministry for more than fifty years, and his track record proves that he's been right on. He's a good example.

Brother Hagin says humorously that if he'd had his way, he'd go sit by a creek and eat wild onions (or be unknown and live a simple life). But the Spirit of God has anointed his lips, and *there are things he must command in the spirit realm.* In the natural realm, generals deal with generals, and so forth. It is the same in the spirit realm.

A Characteristic of Grief

The sixth characteristic of a true prophet is: *Prophets are saddened by what grieves God.* They have the heart and pulse of God, so of course what grieves God grieves them.

I didn't understand that truth for years. Early in my ministry, when I would become *grieved,* I would think that the *depression* my mother had suffered from was coming on me. (I didn't know how to discern between spiritual grief and natural depression.)

Sometimes I'd be in a meeting, ready to prophesy, and all of a sudden I'd become grieved. Maybe the music would be totally wrong because the musicians were not in tune with God; they hadn't spent time in prayer.

Once I was supposed to hold a meeting in a certain church, but God said, "Don't go to that meeting."

I found out they had dancers in their services — you know, women on tippy toes prancing around. Although there is a place for drama in the church, we're getting into things that sadden and grieve God.

Music, dance, or anything else that calls attention to the person, not to God, *grieves* Him — and I don't care how good the performance is.

When I've been in churches that have dancers, I've sat

Characteristics of a True Prophet

on the platform and watched the men when those women danced — and those men weren't worshipping God!

Why! Because the dancers wear skimpy little dresses and you can see everything. (Come to think of it, I've never seen a 500-pound woman among the dancers in those churches. They always get the skinny ones up there.) And their actions grieve God. We've got to bring in true worship that won't grieve Him.

So prophets are moody. Prophets are different. You can go all the way through the Bible and see that prophets are a different breed of person. Often they act depressed or saddened. "Grieved" is a better word.

Being a prophet isn't an excuse to be crabby in the flesh, but when a prophet is grieved, he gets moody. If they're not careful, prophets of God can become depressed. That's why we need to pray for prophets of God. They must learn, as I finally did, to discern between spiritual grief and natural depression.

I often get grieved. That means I've got to go apart and pray to find out what is grieving God. Then I've got to change it in the spirit realm. Things must be *right* for a prophet to operate without hindrance.

I've been in meetings where I knew that the Spirit of God wanted a prophet to get over into the prophet's ministry. He was ready to go over into it, yet it didn't happen. Why? Because the atmosphere wasn't right, or someone did something that quenched the Spirit.

A Characteristic of Intercession

The seventh characteristic of a true propher is: *Prophets are men of deep intercession.*

Jesus is our example as an Intercessor. Intercession starts only when the spirit of intercession comes on you. Like Jesus, prophets often will go off by themselves to pray. That's why you must leave them alone sometimes: They need to get off by themselves and intercede.

Often deep intercession will hit me if I'm praying for someone. I was standing behind a fellow minister in a prayer line the other night. When his anointing would start to wane, deep intercession would hit me, and I'd have to intercede for him. The anointing would come on him stronger. Later, when I was ministering, he did the same thing for me. We are old friends, and we know we need each other in the Body of Christ.

In intercession, the prophet not only speaks to God about men; he speaks to men about God. For example, in Exodus 32:7-42, Moses interceded for the children of Israel. And the great prophet Samuel was inconsolable at King Saul's downfall:

> **Then came the word of the Lord unto Samuel, saying,**
>
> **It repenteth me that I have set up Saul to be king: for he is turned back from following me, and hath not performed my commandments. And it grieved Samuel; and he cried unto the Lord all night.**
>
> 1 Samuel 15:10, 11

A Characteristic of Hope

The eighth characteristic of a true prophet is, *he is a man of expectation, faith, and hope.* We've all heard prophets of gloom and doom. All they speak is damnation and doom. Don't listen to them!

Some of them have prophesied that California is going to fall into the ocean, and the new beach is going to be in Arizona! Every time California has an earthquake, here come the doomsday prophets, shaking their heads and saying, "Yeah, the Big One's coming!"

California isn't going anywhere. There are a lot of covenant people out there.

You also must watch out for the prophet who prophesies in vain to you. They're the ones who try to get you to walk in vanity. They say, "Thus saith the Lord, you're going to be a great man (or woman) of God." Remember: Without God, you're nothing. I was nothing when God got hold of me, but in Him I am the righteousness of God.

A true prophet of God may give you a warning from God, but he also will give you light — the revelation or answer for how you can change the thing God showed him.

The true prophet is also a man of *restoration:* Like Daniel and Moses, he brings us back to God, and he brings God back to us. The prophet brings God back to the Body of Christ. There's just something about a prophet: He can get before God and say, "Remember your Covenant!"

That's one reason why prophets are so important to the Body of Christ today. That's why we need more and more intercession for the prophet's ministry. There's a church I know of that comes together once a week just to pray for the prophets in the land. They pray that the prophets will come forth and say what God wants them to say.

Even if their message *sounds* negative, there will always be faith and hope in messages delivered by true prophets, because they produce faith and hope. The Bible says if you listen to the prophets, you'll *prosper,* and that's true:

. . . Believe in the Lord your God, so shall ye be established; believe his prophets, so shall ye prosper.

2 Chronicles 20:20

Notice it says *"believe* his prophets." Believe them! You will prosper by listening to prophets.

Several years ago, many prophets prophesied, "Be careful in the next two years. Don't get too far in debt." Those who didn't listen to them went ahead, got in debt, and many lost everything they had.

I got up to preach one Sunday morning in Los Angeles and all of a sudden I prophesied that gold was going to double in value. And it did.

The Prophet: Friend of God

You'll remember that Brother Hagin said at his 1987 Campmeeting that if Christians don't pray, and if the wrong man becomes President of the United States, the economy of this country will be in a big mess.

Some will argue, "Well, I don't care about the economy. God is going to take care of me." That's being selfish. It would be difficult for you and other Christians to preach the Gospel and live in peace if your bills weren't paid.

When the prophets of the land start getting blessed and make changes by the spirit of God, the rest of the Body will be blessed and will turn, too, because the prophets lead the Body.

A Characteristic of Humility

The ninth characteristic of a true prophet is that *he is a man of meekness and humility.* He never conveys the impression that he's infallible.

One thing that saddens God is when we give men all the glory. We can have heroes, but we must be careful that we don't *worship* the leaders of great movements. If we do, we'll start seeing their crowds dwindle, because God is the One who must get *all* the glory.

The true prophet always gives the impression that he is willing to have his life, his ministry, and the way he operates in the gifts be evaluated and judged.

In First Corinthians 14:29, Paul writes about prophets judging things that are done in services: "Let the prophets speak two or three, and let the others judge."

Then he says in First Thessalonians:

> **Quench not the Spirit.**
> **Despise not prophesyings.**
> **Prove all things; hold fast that which is good.**
> **Abstain from all appearance of evil.**
>
> **1 Thessalonians 5:19-22**

Chapter 2
"I Ordained Thee a Prophet"

Any study of the office of prophet must include an examination of how a prophet is called.

The most important thing to consider is this: It is imperative that you know beyond any doubt that you are called of God to be a prophet. Your call must be confirmed until absolutely no doubt remains in your mind because, as James says, "A double minded man is unstable in all his ways" (James 1:8).

If I were on an operating table and a qualified doctor came in, saying, "Well, I don't know if I can do this or not," I'd yell, "Get this guy out of here!" He'd better have confidence in what he's doing before he operates on *me*!

Regardless of the call on your life, it's essential that you have complete assurance about your ministry. Many of you went to Bible school to find out. You felt a call, or you had an urge to do something for God. It usually takes a while for that urge to progress to the point of total assurance.

You can know if you have a divine call by *conviction*, by a *witness* in your spirit, and by a divine *compulsion* on the inside of you concerning the call that's upon your life. You can even know if you're called to be a prophet or not. It's the same way you can tell if you're a pastor or not:

The characteristics of that mantle will be on you!

Prophecy Confirms, Never Calls

Here are some additional warnings and guidelines you

can use to tell if you're really called into the ministry:

If someone prophesies that you are called to the fivefold ministry, but God hasn't told you, disregard the prophecy!

Sometimes I'll enter a church and a young man will get me in a corner, or slip into the pastor's office and whisper, "I'm a prophet."

I always reply, "Oh yeah? How do you know?"

He'll say, "Well, a guy here prophesied, or someone came through and prophesied over me that I'm a prophet. Uh, what do you *do* as a prophet?"

"Well, I *work*. I work in the Gospel. I don't sit up on a mountaintop and prophesy all the time."

"Huh?"

The true New Testament gift of prophecy only *confirms*; it never *calls*. When people started prophesying over me about the different callings on my life, I already kind of knew about them. The whole picture was still fuzzy to me, but their words confirmed what God was already dealing with me about.

Needs vs. Calls

Know something else: *A need is not a call.* Some people see a need, so they try to call themselves into the ministry in order to fulfill that need. In other words, just because they are *burdened* for Mexican orphans doesn't mean they are *called* to be a missionary to Mexico.

If you enter the ministry and God didn't call you, you will fail. But if you have that divine call, know it, and remain faithful to it, you will succeed.

I've known young men who have wanted to get involved in the ministry. They've said, "God told me to do this for you. God told me to do that for you." But after a while, when the going got tough, off they went. They weren't called.

Then I've known people who have said, "Man, it's been so *easy* for me to be in the ministry. I just float from one blessing to the next." I even heard one speaker say, "The devil never bothers me."

I thought, "I must be doing something wrong!" I've never had it that easy. I've had to fight for everything that I've gotten — fight in prayer and intercession in the spirit realm.

The Fight for Your Ministry

The devil will fight you for that call of God that's on your life.

He will try to talk you out of it.

He doesn't want you in the position that God put you in.

Furthermore, the ministry is not easy — I don't care what anyone tells you. Believe me, there will be rough times, but you must remain faithful to your call during those times. You see, there's a price you pay to walk in the anointing!

You may be called upon to make great sacrifices, but the call alone will pull you through if you remain faithful. That's one way you can tell if you've got the call: Just remain faithful to it, and that call will pull you through.

I had a rough time getting into the ministry. Every time I look back on my life, even on the tragedies, I say, "But I made it!"

If you think you are called to stand in a particular office, wait and test your call to find out for sure. Even if you are called to one of the ministry gifts, you won't step into it immediately; you'll start at the bottom.

If God exposed you to the full power of the office while you're still in training, it could destroy you and your ministry. You haven't learned how to be faithful yet. You haven't learned how to be consecrated yet.

Can you imagine a little baby playing in his crib with an H-Bomb? What if his daddy gave it to him and said,

"Now, just push that button, and you'll have all the power you want." It's the same with the fivefold ministries: There's a lot of power in them, and it takes time — years, in fact — to learn how to operate them.

The Years of Preparation

When I was just starting out in the ministry, I was in a morning teaching service, and the power of God fell. I told a young man what God was showing me about him. Later, I felt I had grieved the Spirit of God.

I asked, "What is it, Lord?"

He said, "You shouldn't have told him. I revealed it to you, but you weren't to tell it now. You could hurt him, because he's so enthusiastic. But he'll be all right. You pray for him."

That's how I learned that there's a time to reveal things by the Spirit, and there's a time not to say those things.

Brother Hagin was in the ministry for eighteen years before he entered into the prophet's ministry, but that office didn't come on him until he had been in the ministry for eighteen years!

If you are called to the fivefold ministry, use your years of preparation to study. Preparation time is never lost time. Whatever your call is, you *must* build your ministry on the Word of God. You cannot build a ministry on the supernatural, or on a gift. If you will build your ministry on the Word of God, it will last forever, because the Word is forever.

In the future, if sickness and disease come knocking on your door, and if the gifts of the Spirit are not in operation for some reason, you're going to have to stand on the Word. And what if there's no prophet in town?

So, dedicate, consecrate, and submit yourself to God's will in your life. Know that if God *calls* you, He will *equip* you to carry out that call. Your gift *will* make a way for you.

Also, get involved in a local church. Do whatever your hands find to do in the ministry of helps.

Dusting the Pulpit

I'll never forget the night I was dusting the pulpit, and all of a sudden a voice boomed out of the pulpit, saying, "You'll go all over the world and preach." I jumped! No one was around.

I thought my pastor was playing a practical joke on me, so I walked over to the loudspeakers and inspected them. But it was God speaking to me.

I replied, "God, I can't even get up and give a testimony, let alone preach! That ain't my calling. I'm a helper. I work with my hands. I can build buildings, and I can clean toilets. But I can't preach.

Even my pastor told me, "Ed, you'd have to go to speech classes for ten years before you could preach." If I'd have listened to him, I wouldn't be in the ministry today. But here I am, mistakes and all. I was faithful where I was, and a faithful man shall abound in the blessings of God.

As you remain faithful wherever you're at, God will bring you to the top, too. It happens every time. Cream always rises!

Called From My Mother's Womb

Yes, there are times when my knees shake when I get up to preach. However, I *know* what God has called me to do.

The Bible tells us in Isaiah and Jeremiah that a prophet is called from his mother's womb. One day the Lord gave me a vision of my whole life and revealed to me that I, too, was called from the womb. He explained my whole life up to that point in time.

For years, I hadn't realized that the prophet's mantle was upon me. This knowledge gradually unfolded to me.

Things started happening, and God dealt with me about the anointing on my life. However, I didn't understand much about it, because there was a lack of teaching on the office of prophet in those days.

Different men of God like Dick Mills would come to town, call me out of the congregation, and prophesy about my ministry, but I was still in the ministry of helps then. I had the ministry of toilets.

That's right — for five years I cleaned the church toilets. Not too many ministers want to start out by cleaning toilets, but God's got to find out if you're faithful. *If you can't clean toilets for God, how are you going to prophesy for Him?* I hope you don't have to do that, but I was in bad shape.

When the Lord started dealing with me about ministry, I reminded Him, "Lord, I'm not an eloquent speaker." I could never get up and give a talk in grammar school, junior high, or high school (which I didn't finish). There were too many problems at home. My home was full of alcoholism, and I couldn't study under those circumstances, so I dropped out of school.

Several years ago, when the Lord gave me that vision of my life, He said, "Ed Dufresne, I know you. I ordained you and I sanctified you in your mother's womb to be a minister of the Gospel."

Angels Halted My Abortion

In the vision, He showed me that my parents had decided to abort me a few weeks after I had been conceived! That was in 1940. My mother was 15. My dad was just 16. That's pretty young. And World War II was about to break out.

My dad was an apprentice sheet metal man, and he couldn't afford to get married. So they talked about aborting me, and my mother was ready to go for the abortion.

And I saw what happened: I saw angels come down

from heaven and stop it, because God commanded that I was ordained of God. The angels turned the situation around and my parents got married instead of having the abortion.

I was born in June 1941. I'm here. But if they had aborted me, I'd still be a human being, and I'd be in heaven now.

Let's take a little side trip here. When you get to heaven, you're going to see all the aborted children. They're there. Once when God was dealing with me about an unwed mothers' home, I had a vision and saw these aborted children in heaven.

I also saw the women who had aborted their children. They thought they had gotten rid of them. It's absolutely shocking to me that even Christian women get abortions. Some of them, of course, later repent, and they can be set free of their sin and guilt.

I saw as the saved women walked through the gates of heaven, and there their little aborted children were, saying, "Mommy, I love you!"

That's the mercy and love of God! You know, parents can misuse or beat a child, and he'll still stick up for his parents. A judge may ask him, "Did your mommy and daddy do that?"

"No, my mommy and daddy didn't do it." That's why we ought to be like a child: They're very forgiving. Of such is the kingdom of heaven, Jesus said.

Until the Lord showed me this vision, I had never known that my parents had considered aborting me. Later, I asked my dad about it. He said, "Yes, sorry to say, that's true. We were going to abort you."

The Devil's Plot Against Prophets

The Lord revealed many other things to me. He went all the way through my life and showed me everything, explaining why things had happened and why people had behaved as they had.

I had many relatives on both sides of the family who were in mental institutions. When my grandfather found out my mother was pregnant with me, he committed suicide. He left a note to my mother, telling her that's the reason he committed suicide — he couldn't handle her pregnancy. He felt degraded by her actions.

Then, of course, my mother had to live with that guilt the rest of her life, and that's what drove her into mental institutions.

My parents vowed they weren't going to become alcoholics. But after my brother was born, they started sipping little cocktails and having a little wine, and they did end up as alcoholics.

All of these things were geared to destroy that anointing that came out of my mother's womb — her son who was ordained a prophet.

Know this: The devil hates anointed men and women of God. He hates Christians, period, and he seems to particularly want to destroy prophets!

Look at Brother Hagin's life. He was born prematurely. He didn't even look like a human baby. The doctor and his Grandmother Drake couldn't detect any signs of life, so his grandmother put him in a shoe box and was going to bury him in the back yard!

But His angels intervened to protect the prophet's anointing, and his grandmother suddenly detected a little movement in the tiny body. And he's still alive, 70-some years later!

I appreciated God so much for taking me all the way back through my life and explaining everything that has happened to me. I learned that all the bad things were engineered by the devil to destroy the anointing that has been on my life from my mother's womb.

"I Ordained Thee a Prophet"

The devil is working overtime to destroy the anointing on the lives of *all* of God's servants. That's why we shouldn't get angry at the person who has fallen to Satan's wiles. We have no right to criticize such a person. We don't know all the stress and strain he has been under. We should just keep quiet and pray for him.

God's Call to Isaiah and Jeremiah

The Lord gave much the same commission to the prophet Isaiah that He did to Jeremiah:

> Listen, O isles, unto me; and hearken, ye people, from far; The Lord hath called me from the womb; from the bowels of my mother hath he made mention of my name.
>
> And he hath made my mouth like a sharp sword; in the shadow of his hand hath he hid me, and made me a polished shaft; in his quiver hath he hid me;
>
> And said unto me, Thou art my servant, O Israel, in whom I will be glorified.
>
> Isaiah 49:1-3

The following passage from Jeremiah reveals how God looks at His prophets. This is the assurance He gave the prophet Jeremiah:

> Before I formed thee in the belly I knew thee; and before thou camest forth out of the womb I sanctified thee, and I ordained thee a prophet unto the nations.
>
> Then said I, Ah, Lord God! behold, I cannot speak: for I am a child.
>
> But the Lord said unto me, Say not, I am a child: for thou shalt go to all that I shall send thee, and whatsoever I command thee thou shalt speak.
>
> Be not afraid of their faces: for I am with thee to deliver thee, saith the Lord.
>
> Then the Lord put forth his hand, and touched

my mouth. And the Lord said unto me, Behold, I have put my words in thy mouth.

See, I have this day set thee over the nations and over the kingdoms, to root out, and to pull down, and to destroy, and to throw down, to build, and to plant.

Jeremiah 1:5-10

Let's begin with the fifth verse: *"Before I formed thee* in the belly *I knew thee;* and before thou camest forth out of the womb I sanctified thee. . . ."

Isn't it amazing that people will abort children? Their excuse is, "Well, that was nothing but a *blob."* But here God says, "I knew them before they were even formed. In the belly I knew them." *You don't know a blob!*

"And before thou camest forth out of the womb I sanctified thee. . . ." This means that God set the prophet apart. *". . . and I ordained thee a prophet* unto the nations." (Did you know there are different degrees of prophets? Some prophets are appointed over specific cities or nations.)

"And God Hath Set Some in the Church"

First of all, God is the One who calls someone to the ministry. *God* does this — not dad, mom, family, or a church board. You can't set yourself apart as a prophet or any other gift ministry. You've got to be commissioned or ordained by God.

I believe in the fivefold ministries that scripture tells us *God sets* in the Church of the Lord Jesus Christ:

> **AND GOD HATH SET SOME IN THE CHURCH,** first apostles, secondarily prophets, thirdly teachers, after that miracles, then gifts of healings, helps, governments, diversities of tongues.
>
> 1 Corinthians 12:28
>
> AND HE GAVE SOME, apostles; and some, prophets; and some, evangelists; and some, pas-

tors and teachers;

> For the perfecting of the saints, for the work of the ministry, for the edifying of the body of Christ.
>
> Ephesians 4:11, 12

One day I was reading First Corinthians 12:28, and I asked the Lord, "What do You mean by 'set'?" My mind immediately went back to the years I was in construction work. I know what happens when concrete sets up.

When we poured concrete and it was still wet, we could move it around, but once it was *set*, we couldn't move it unless we dynamited it. This is God's plan for the Church: He sets ministries in place.

It amazes me that people think they can call themselves into the ministry! I saw a TV preacher who said, "Bless God, if we need a prophet in our church, God will anoint *me* to be the prophet, and if we need an apostle, He'll anoint *me* to be the apostle."

I thought, "How ignorant can you get? That isn't what the Bible says." The Bible says, "And God hath set some in the church. . . ."

Men cannot set the fivefold ministries in the Body of Christ.

Something New: Resident Prophets

It is God's desire to have the entire fivefold ministry operating in the local church. However, the leadership should not *appoint* the fivefold gifts into their church; they should allow God to place them into their positions. Yet I see a very great error abroad right now in the Body of Christ. What is happening is that men with good intentions, who are trying to go along with what they think the Bible says, are electing someone who prophesies as their prophet — with disastrous results. They're also taking it upon themselves — in the flesh — to set their own apostles in their churches.

The Prophet: Friend of God

I've been in churches where people pointed out certain men and said, "This is our apostle, and this is our apostle, and this is our *resident prophet.*"

I don't know why, but many of the so-called prophets are big old guys. They sit on the platform looking *gruff* — for that's how they think a prophet should look — and they strut around self-importantly, saying, "Thus saith the Lord. . . ." No, thus saith *them!* They're not true prophets. I call them "hireling prophets."

Once when someone said, "He's a resident prophet," God said to me, "No, he isn't. *Men set him in there*, because they're trying to set up the New Testament Church."

How to Create False Prophets

Unless God sets a prophet in a church, you'll have a false prophet! Only God can set a prophet in the Church.

I've seen shipwreck in people's lives because of these "resident prophets." The church leaders have told them, "You're our resident prophet — now prophesy!" So they've "prophesied": "Thus saith the Lord, give me your house." Or, "Thus saith the Lord, you married the wrong person. You're to leave your husband and go with me or someone else."

That's nothing but a bunch of trash. But there are people who would rather hear the lies of false prophets than hear the truth. They want to hear what they want to hear.

The Prophet's Strength

Jeremiah protested, "Ah, Lord God! behold, I cannot speak: for I am a child. But the Lord said unto me, Say not, I am a child: for thou shalt go to all that I shall send thee, and whatsoever I command thee thou shalt speak" (vv. 6, 7).

That's a strong word. There's something about a prophet under the anointing of God: When he says something that

God commands, it's stronger. It goes deeper into the spirit realm. It can change cities.

I didn't even know these verses were in the Bible when God first dealt with me concerning my call. He said to me, "You will obey, and you will command what I tell you."

Verse 8: "Be not afraid of their faces: for I am with thee to deliver thee, saith the Lord."

Sometimes a prophet needs to be delivered from the fear of what people will say. This doesn't happen overnight, however. I'm almost there, but not quite.

Three years ago it got me in trouble. God dealt with me about it in Israel. He told me, "You've been afraid of man, and sometimes you'll hesitate and back off because of criticism and what people say."

Whatever ministry you're in (or even if you're not in the ministry), you're not to be afraid of other people's opinions. In other words, don't let people talk you out of your healing, your prosperity, your calling, or whatever.

Verse 9: "Then the Lord put forth his hand, and touched my mouth. [I remember when God did that to me.] And the Lord said unto me, Behold, I have put my words in thy mouth." When God touches your mouth, your mouth is never the same!

The Prophets: Wrecking and Construction

Verse 10 illustrates why it is essential that pastors recognize the prophet's ministry and invite prophets to come to their churches: "See, I have this day set thee over the nations and over the kingdoms, *to root out,* and *to pull down,* and *to destroy,* and *to throw down, to build,* and *to plant.*"

As this verse points out so eloquently, prophets *root out, pull down, destroy, throw down, build,* and *plant.* That means they root things out that need to be rooted out — evil spirits, religious teachings, and whatever else needs to be changed — and the whole direction of that church can be corrected.

Notice what else prophets do: They build and plant! After they "clean house," they leave a church in better condition than when they came. That's one reason why God set this mantle in the Body of Christ.

A prime example of a prophet's ministry being exercised this way publicly took place in a recent meeting in Tulsa. Brother Hagin said by the Spirit that there was a pastor present who was so discouraged by the behavior of certain men on his board that he was about to resign.

Brother Hagin gave the first names of the three troublemakers; then he advised the pastor not to quit, because God was going to turn the situation around.

That brought light. It brought revelation and straightened things out. It wasn't negative. Brother Hagin nailed the devil and a bunch of deacons, glory to God!

It was done publicly, but as we saw earlier, a prophet does not necessarily have to prophesy publicly in order to be effective. A prophet can be in his prayer time. He can be in his own bedroom. He can be in the bathroom. When that prophetic anointing comes on him, things will be said by the Spirit of God that can change cities, nations, kingdoms, and other aspects of the spirit realm.

The Prophets as Warriors

For example, the prophet may come to your city and immediately start to engage in spiritual warfare with the satanic ruler or rulers over that city. Why? Because the prophet's anointing is deeper and stronger than most anointings, and it can defeat those powerful demonic entities.

Perhaps the Christians in that city had been praying for years, trying to pull down that deeply entrenched stronghold. Sometimes it takes a big guy to knock out a big guy.

It's the same in the spirit realm: God's generals deal

with Satan's generals, lieutenants battle lieutenants, corporals fight corporals, captains engage captains, and so forth. Regular intercession can't handle everything. That's another reason why we need the prophet's ministry.

You pastors need to teach your people about the prophet's ministry before he arrives at your church. There will be things he will discern almost immediately in the spirit realm and want uprooted in your church and over your city.

If you teach them well, your people will know how to "pull" on the prophet's gift. They'll know what to do and what *not* to do when his gift goes into operation.

If pastors would discern the prophet's ministry and have prophets in their churches, there wouldn't be as many messes in the Church as there are.

A pastor told me his church was going down the tubes. He invited me to minister there. Afterwards, he wrote me, saying, "I don't know what happened, but as a result of some of the things you said, our finances have changed. There's also a stronger healing anointing in the church."

What happened? The Lord revealed some things by the Spirit of God that needed to be rooted out. There were some things in the spirit realm that had to be dealt with through the prophet's anointing.

Yes, the Holy Spirit is our Teacher and our Guide and, yes, teaching is valid — don't misunderstand me — but the teacher's anointing wouldn't have been effective in that case. It required the prophet's anointing, which is a stronger, different anointing. When you wear that mantle, you can go into the spirit realm and deal with those satanic forces.

Prophets and Teachers

In the next few years, prophets will be speaking revelation that teachers can then build upon. There are certain things that still need to be said by the Spirit of God. And unless the teachers hear these things, their messages will simply be copies of other teachers' messages.

Several years ago I heard one speaker say some things I didn't understand at the time; his statements seemed to contradict each other. He said, "We really don't need a revival in our churches today as much as we need the prophet's ministry to come forth. Now, we *do* need revival in our churches," he added, "but when the prophets come and speak, that will bring revival."

I believe we're going to start seeing this. Some of the prophets are going to start teaching on this. They're going to start rooting out and pulling down. Churches will change.

The pastors will start saying, "We don't understand it. You got up here under the anointing of God and spoke some things and — boom! — things changed. The finances changed. Things changed spiritually. Sister Bucketmouth finally repented. I've been reading the Word. We've had people here praying night and day, in deep intercession. What happened?"

That's the ministry of a prophet. Do you understand the importance of it? The devil does. He's been trying to kill the prophets — he's been trying to get some of them to go home before their time — but now the true prophets are coming on the scene, and they're going to obey God.

The true prophets will say things by the Spirit that we'll use to build a foundation to ride on into this next wave.

We read where Jeremiah was told he would root out, pull down, destroy, and throw down. But he was also told that prophets build and plant. The Church will build and plant on the foundation established by the prophets.

Prophets as Seers

In verse 11, the Lord asks the prophet, "Jeremiah, what *seeth* thou?" Jeremiah replies, "I see a rod of an almond tree. Then said the Lord unto me, Thou hast well seen: for I will hasten my word to perform it. And the word of the Lord came unto me the second time, saying, "What *seeth* thou? . . ." (vv. 12, 13).

Remember, the prophet is a seer, He *sees* things. We could say, as some do, "The prophet is the eye of the Body of Christ." What prophets see, they tell the Body of Christ. *When a seer sees something and then speaks it, God will perform it.* That's why the prophet's words won't fall to the ground.

Often God will give the prophet a word of knowledge in vision form. For example, I've read how Brother Hagin was in the Spirit and dealt with cancers on several occasions.

He was caught up by the Spirit into another realm, saw or discerned the evil spirit hanging onto its victim, and dealt with it. The demon left, and the person was delivered. When he dealt with cancer demons in these visions, all the people were healed.

When this has happened to me, I, too, have had a hundred percent success rate.

Prophetic Warning

I would prefer to use someone else as an example, but this actually happened to me: One Sunday morning I was preaching in my former church in California, and I went out in the Spirit and saw that someone was going to try to kill the President of the United States. I told the congregation, "Pray, pray, pray!" We were able to deal with it in the spirit realm.

Soon after this, I flew to a meeting in Texas, and I was in a room with Norvel Hayes when we heard that a young man had tried to assassinate our President. He didn't succeed.

Can you imagine what would happen if we did away with the prophet's ministry? What God revealed that morning brought light and illumination.

The Prophet: Friend of God

We read in Amos 3:7, "Surely the Lord God will do nothing but he revealeth his secret unto his servants the prophets." *Unless the Lord reveals it to the prophets, He won't do anything.* He will do *nothing* unless He reveals it to His prophets. That's what I mean about the light coming to the Body of Christ.

It was like the Lord told Jeremiah, "Thou hast well *seen:* for I will hasten my word to *perform* it." Or, "You *saw* rightly, and I will *perform* it." If the prophets don't see and speak it out, how is God going to perform it?

What, then, is the meaning of the almond tree Jeremiah saw? An almond tree is one of the first trees to show life in the spring. It starts budding before anything else.

What is God talking about? He's saying, "I am showing you some things *before* they happen." That's the job of the watchman on the tower. (If the watchman doesn't have any light, how are the people going to have light?) That's also the job of the prophet.

The Prophets: Eye of God

I believe we can see this stated as a paralled truth in Luke 11:

> **No man, when he hath lighted a candle, putteth it in a secret place, neither under a bushel, but on a candlestick, that they which come in may see the light.**
>
> **The light of the body is the eye: therefore when thine eye is single, thy whole body also is full of light; but when thine eye is evil, thy body also is full of darkness.**
>
> **Take heed therefore that the light which is in thee be not darkness.**
>
> **Luke 11:33-35**

The prophet is the eye, bringing light to the Body of Christ. When the prophet speaks, he brings light and revelation for the whole Body, giving direction. Then, as we saw earlier, the teachers will build on that foundation the prophet has laid.

Of course, we are not led by prophecy; nor are we led by prophets. We are led by God's Spirit and His Word. On the other hand, the Bible says that if we believe His prophets, we shall prosper. Furthermore, we can be led into the light that a prophet brings by the Spirit of God. You've got to weigh it out.

Bear in mind that a prophet must be proven, mature, and walking obediently before the Lord with a pure heart. Also, a true prophet should prophesy in line with the Word of God. If what he says *isn't* in line with the Word of God, you don't want to listen to him.

I judge the things prophets and others say according to the Word of God. I also judge the "fruit" in the person's life. No, I'm not talking about the kind of clothes he wears or the kind of car he drives. I'm talking about his spiritual track record. Is he seasoned? Does he have the right kind of character? What about his love — does he walk in love?

If a prophet is rebellious, I don't want to hear him. If he's one of the little "hot airs" going around watching X-rated movies and living in the world, I'm not going to listen to him. He can't be a prophet and have a worldly spirit. That harlot, the world, will get your power!

Darkness or Light?

True prophets *are* speaking today, but if the Body of Christ refuses to listen or obey, we're going to be in darkness and bondage.

If the Church only realized that the prophet brings light to set you free, not put you in bondage! Too many are saying, "Well, we're not led by prophets — and anyway, we don't like what that prophet said."

True prophecy enhances and confirms the Word of God; it never violates or contradicts it. Also, true prophecy produces a new flow of life, not bondage.

Prophets only *confirm* what God has already been speaking to us. It is true that the Holy Spirit reveals everything we need to know, and it is true that we have an anointing from the Holy One to know all things (1 John 2:20); but the prophet has "spiritual binoculars" that allow him to see with clarity and definition.

How to Miss the Voice of God

We often close our ears to sensitive areas in our life, for the flesh wars against the things of the Spirit. So God in His wisdom has the prophet speak what we don't want to hear. There are little adjustments that we need to make, and the prophet helps us make them. Those who are full of darkness don't want the light, because they would have to correct some of their pet practices.

I wonder how many movements of God we've already missed because the Church would not listen, preferring to continue in their rebellion. That's why there are all kinds of dead denominational churches on every corner. They didn't listen to the prophets of the land and build on the new foundation they were trying to lay. Sixty years have gone by, and those dead churches remain unchanged.

Or they lacked discernment and listened to the wrong prophet. "We're going to follow this prophet," they said, "and he'll lead us up in the mountains, and we'll store food." I'm not talking about that kind of a foundation.

I don't know how people get so dippy! I've never seen so many "dipsticks" in the Body of Christ as there are today, despite all the good teaching that is going out.

How to Miss the Call of God

If you are a dippy, half-dedicated Christian who is messing around with the things of this world, you won't be conscious of God speaking to your spirit — and you could very easily miss the call of God!

And don't tell me, "Well, I know I'm a prophet, so I'm just going to sit in my room and pray all the time. I'm not getting involved in anything. I'm a prophet."

You don't start at the top, honey. I cleaned toilets for five years — remember?

Furthermore, if you start playing with worldly things, such as watching sports or movies all the time, and you don't spend time before God and get involved in church and with the things of God, you could miss the call of God!

Chapter 3
Different Ranks and Different Anointings

Before a minister can press further into the spirit realm, he or she must first be equipped to do so.

Everyone thinks a minister can do everything, but he can't. Ministers in the modern Church, however, are trying to be jacks-of-all-trades.

A minister can get off by getting into activities that God never called him to do; even spiritual activities. Therefore, it's important to find out exactly what God has called you to do, and then do it. Remain in your place, or rank, in the Body of Christ.

Any ministry gift carries different ranks within that office. Romans 12 bears that out. We'll start by studying the first verse:

> I beseech you therefore, brethren, by the mercies of God, that ye PRESENT YOUR BODIES A LIVING SACRIFICE, holy, acceptable unto God, which is your reasonable service.

Paul is talking about ministry gifts here. Just a few verses before, in Romans 11:29, he said, "For the gifts and calling of God are without repentance."

Once God calls you — once He gives you that gift — He won't take it back. Therefore, Paul tells us here how to maintain the anointing on a ministry.

The Minister: A Living Sacrifice

First, Paul says, you must give your body up as "a living sacrifice."

This is my twenty-fifth year of ministry. When I first got saved, as I mentioned before, I started in the toilet ministry. But that was a ministry, and the time I spent in the ministry of helps wasn't lost time. It was preparation time. I learned a lot cleaning toilet and dealing with people!

For the past twenty years, I've been in a traveling ministry. Some of you know what it's like to travel all the time. At church, you may enjoy a heavy anointing, with people being healed, big crowds, and everything going well.

But the next morning when you wake up in your hotel room, you don't even feel saved! You look at yourself in the mirror and say, "Hey, *you're* the righteousness of God." And your body speaks up, "You sure don't *look* like it."

That's when you walk by faith. You can't walk by the anointing that's on you in the services. That's when you have to give up your body as a living sacrifice.

Hotel rooms all look alike. They all smell alike. Some of them are just nicer than others, but they're all the same. You get so tired of those four walls! During the day, you pace back and forth, praying, looking at those walls.

Dead Men

I once asked myself, "What am I *doing,* living in a hotel room? I could be home with my wife and my son!"

And the Spirit of the Lord rose up in my spirit and said, *"Dead men don't gripe."*

You know what happens to a living sacrifice? It dies.

Dead men never fight back, either. So if you're going to make it in the ministry, you can't complain, "So-and-so stepped on my toes." "So-and-so said this or that about me"

Different Ranks and Different Anointings

Dead men never get even. Have you ever been in a mortuary and seen a dead man jump out of his coffin, yelling, "You own me $150"? You never get even in the ministry either.

Prophets must give up their bodies as a living sacrifice. Even today they throw stones at prophets.

Some of you say, "Yes, I want the prophet's ministry." Will you still want it when things like this happen? Will you still be willing to "present your bodies a living sacrifice, holy, acceptable unto God, which is your reasonable service"?

Two Requirements for Ministry

Paul continues in verse 2, "And be not conformed to this world: but be ye transformed by the renewing of your mind, that ye may prove what is that good, and acceptable, and perfect, will of God."

So there are two things you've got to do to be in the ministry:

First, give your body up as a living sacrifice for what you're called to do, making whatever sacrifice it takes to walk in that calling.

But people don't want to pay that sacrifice. They don't want to pay that preparation time. They don't want to pay that price. They want to jump right into their ministry.

They don't want to carry another man's coat in the ministry of helps. "Yeah, well maybe I'll do it for a year or two, but not for ten years!"

See, you don't want to give up your body as a living sacrifice. You want to do what *you* want to do instead of what God's telling you to do.

Second, renew your mind with the Word of God concerning your calling.

Finding God's Perfect Will

Notice what the Word says will happen when you do these two things: ". . . that ye may prove what is that good, and acceptable, and perfect, will of God." That's how you're going to do the perfect will of God in your calling! Many people just do good works in their calling. They never get to the perfect will of God in their calling.

When Jesus appeared to Brother Hagin years ago, He said, "Most of my ministers don't even get to the first phase of their ministry." Can you imagine that — they don't even get to the *first* phase! That means, of course, that there are different phases you go through in the ministry.

I want to do the perfect will of God and go through every phase that God has for me in my ministry.

People pray, "O Lord, I want to do miracles!" *Why* do you want to do miracles? Do you want people to look at you and say, "Isn't he a hero?" You're going to have to pay a price if you want to do miracles.

Paul's Recipe for Success

Paul continues in verse 3:

> **For I say, through the GRACE given unto me, to every man that is among you, not to think of himself more highly than he ought to think; but to think soberly, according as GOD HATH DEALT TO EVERY MAN THE MEASURE OF FAITH.**

True, we all have the same measure of ordinary, saving faith — I'm not contradicting that — but in this passage of scripture, Paul's also talking about *the measure of faith for ministry*. In other words, because our callings are different, it takes more grace and faith to perform some of them, even as some require different anointings.

I once complained, "Lord, this certain man gets on TV and puts all us faith people down, yet he's got the biggest

Different Ranks and Different Anointings

ministry. How does he get away with it?"

The Lord said, "I gave him *a measure of faith for an evangelist*, to get his job done. Now he has to develop his personal faith."

Paul also mentions " . . . the grace given unto me, to every man that is among you, not to think of himself more highly than he ought. . . ."

Why did Paul mention grace and humility in the same breath? *Because one minister has more grace than another minister to get his job done.* And he's not supposed to think of himself more highly than he thinks of his brother with the smaller ministry. You see, it all originated with God anyway and not with you, so how can you take the credit?

You may say, "I want a big ministry!" Then you'd better have the grace and the measure of faith necessary to run a big ministry and to believe in the finances!

Do you want to know why many ministers get in trouble financially? Because we launch out into a certain project simply because we want to do it, yet God never gave us the grace or measure of faith to do that kind of work.

Herds of Problems

I know, because I started a school in my church in Southern California — grades kindergarten through high school. It caused problem after problem after problem. Parents used to wait outside my office in *herds*, ready to kill me because of something that happened in the school, or because a teacher had spanked their child!

Finally I went into the sanctuary. I said, "God, You are going to have to do something! I'm doing what *You* told me to do."

He said, "I never told you to start a school. You went to a church growth seminar and *they* said that every church should have a school. I never gave you the grace or the measure of faith to start a school."

So that's why I had so many problems! So that's why it was costing so much money! The next day, I cancelled the school — and then big herds of parents gathered outside my back door, mad because I was shutting it down.

I learned the hard way: *You can't go beyond the grace and faith God has given you for your ministry.*

We get in trouble when we add things onto our ministry, saying God told us to do it. I'm talking about the prophet's and the pastor's ministries in particular. This is practical advice.

Measures of Pride

A young pastor friend of mind has a huge new building. It seats 5100 people, and it was filled before it was even completed. Other preachers visit the building and say, "*I'm going to do that!*" No, God has given that young man the grace and the measure of faith to get that job done.

I was at a ministers' convention once and heard the respected pastor of a large church get up and say, "God does not bless storefront churches." And I saw 75 percent of those pastors drop their heads in shame. They were supposed to be there to be helped, not destroyed.

That speaker should never have made that statement, because God has given him grace and a measure of faith to accomplish special things. You're not to judge what God has given other people, just because they've got a smaller measure. "For I say . . . to every man . . . not to think of himself more highly than he ought to think. . . ." Pride will destroy you.

This teaching out of Romans 12 has set many preachers free across this country. They were all thinking, "I'm not having success." I tell them, "Then you're judging success the way the world judges success."

If someone told me, "You're not having success. You built a building that seats 800, and it isn't filled up," I would

Different Ranks and Different Anointings

reply, "Buddy, I'm just obeying God. I did what God said." He said, 'Put 800 chairs in this building.' "

"Well, what do you think is going to happen now?"

"I don't know. I just go day by day. God might say, 'Start a church and give it to someone' — I don't know. I'm just here, working for God."

Success in the Kingdom

When discouraged young pastors tell me, "I'm not doing anything for God," I tell them, "Get in your prayer closet for that grace and that measure of faith you need. If God gives you grace and a measure of faith for only 50 people, you'll find yourself standing beside Dr. Paul Yonggi Cho, pastor of the world's largest church, in the awards ceremony when you get to heaven. The Lord will tell you the same thing He will tell Dr. Cho: 'Well done, thou good and faithful servant.' "

You see, we get in the flesh and look at success the way the world does. Instead, we must walk in what God has called us to do and look at things from the perspective of the kingdom of God.

Not all of you who are reading this book are called into the fivefold ministry, and I understand that, but in order to discuss the prophet's ministry we needed to mention these practical matters. Practical things will produce spiritual things!

So if God tells you to have a television ministry, you need to get in your prayer room, and He'll give you the grace and faith to be able to step out and do it. But if God *hasn't* told you to do that thing that seems so attractive to you, you'd better pray about it first!

Gifts Differing

Paul confirms all of this in the next verses: "For as we have many members in one body, and *all members have the same office. . . . Having then gifts differing* according to the grace that is given to us, whether prophecy, let us prophesy according to the proportion of faith" (vv. 4-6). Notice again that not all members of the Body of Christ hold the same office.

Yet people today are trying to do what they did in David's time: walk in someone else's grace, or imitate what they're doing for God.

David went down to the brook and selected some stones for his slingshot. That was his customary way of fighting, and he had been successful doing it. But King Saul tried to put his own armor — his grace, his measure of faith — on David.

David soon said, "No, it isn't working," so he took off all that armor and picked up those stones again. They represented the grace and the measure of faith God had given *him*.

A Lesson for Prophets

So you prophets quit trying to walk in Brother Hagin's anointing, Brother Copeland's anointing, or someone else's anointing. We've been guilty of this in the Faith Movement.

We've said, "Bless God, if Brother Copeland has an airplane, *I'll* get one." Or, "I'm going to do such and such, too." No, walk in the grace that God has given *you*. The gifts differ, according to the grace that is given to us.

Thousands of people take trips to see Dr. Chao's great work in Korea. You can go over there and get inspired and learn his methods, but to imitate him, you'd better have the same grace and the same measure of faith Dr. Cho has — which his mother-in-law prayed down on him!

Let's look at verse 6 again: "Having then gifts differing according to the grace that is given to us. . . ." The ministry gifts carry different ranks and different anointings. ". . . let us prophesy according to the proportion of faith."

God never gives a minister a bigger call than his gift of faith. As we saw, this "measure of faith" has nothing to do with personal faith; rather, it is the faith given to enable you to perform the work God has called you to do in your rank. No matter what your rank is, you'll be rewarded according to your faithfulness.

Ranking in the Ministry

Ministry ranking is similar to military ranking. The greater you rank within your office, the more people you will affect, either positively or negatively. That's why some people have larger churches than others. They're affecting more people.

When a high-ranking minister is wiped out, all those under him are automatically affected. Therefore, we shouldn't rejoice when one falls and gets hurt, because it will affect all of us in one way or another.

We don't know a man's heart, and we have no right to judge him.

Satan's ranking is parallel with God's ranking, so when one of God's generals knocks out one of Satan's generals, it automatically affects the devils in lower ranks.

The Prophet's Anointing

That's why God gives the prophet a great measure of faith. Every prophet I know has a heavy anointing that was given to him for a reason.

However, in most meetings, people don't even recognize the prophet's anointing when it's present. The prophet's anointing is deeper — it's heavier than other anointings.

I was in a meeting recently, and a heavy anointing came in. The next night, the pastor said, "Well, that was kind of a *low-key* anointing last night. We need to have it more upbeat."

He missed the whole thing! He didn't realize that there was a prophet's anointing in that auditorium! God was dealing with and ministering to thousands of people in that church. Things were being taken care of in the nation by the Spirit of God.

You don't always have to jump up and down, bang and clang, leap onto the chairs, and everything else. There's a time for all that, but there's also a time when God moves quietly and deeply.

Beyond Your Faith

Paul himself could go no further than his measure of faith. That's where a lot of us get in trouble: We go further than what God has called us to do.

For example, if you operate in the gifts, do not feel obligated to "perform" if the anointing isn't there. If the Spirit doesn't manifest, don't try to force something to happen. If you do, you might open yourself up to a familiar spirit, because you'll be off the Word. You won't have that grace and that measure of faith you need to operate in your anointing, so you've opened yourself up to an attack.

Discerning the Lord's Body

According to Ephesians 4:12, 13, God gave the ministry gifts "For the perfecting of the saints, for the work of the ministry, for the edifying of the Body of Christ: Till we all come in the unity of the faith, and of the knowledge of the Son of God, unto a perfect man, unto the measure of the stature of the fulness of Christ."

All the ministry gifts must recognize each other and the part they play in the Body of Christ for this to be accomplished. They must operate in unity.

The apostle inspires and leads us on to fresh conquests

Different Ranks and Different Anointings

for Christ. The prophet speaks secrets and revelations from the throne of God. The evangelist reminds us of lost souls. The pastor recognizes the need to care for new believers. The teacher studies and teaches the prophet's inspired messages.

The eleventh through the fourteenth chapters of First Corinthians talk about discerning the Lord's Body. Notice the following passage.

> **But let a man examine himself, and so let him eat of that bread, and drink of that cup.**
>
> **For he that eateth and drinketh unworthily, eateth and drinketh damnation to himself, not discerning the Lord's body.**
>
> **For this cause many are weak and sickly among you, and many sleep** [die].
>
> **For if we would judge ourselves, we should not be judged.**
>
> 1 Corinthians 11:28-31

There's a triple meaning here when Paul is talking about "discerning the Lord's Body." First, there's the aspect of discerning what was purchased for us on Calvary: salvation, healing, restoration, and so forth.

The second meaning deals with individual members of the Body of Christ correctly discerning *the other members* of the Body.

The third meaning deals with the Body as a whole discerning *the ministry gifts* within the Body.

Paul is saying that you also need to discern the fivefold ministries that God has set into the Body of Christ.

In verse 30, he says the reason why many local churches are weak spiritually, and why many die spiritually, is because they do not discern what God has set in the Church. (The reason why the entire Body of Christ is weak today is because it, too, does not discern or hear what the prophets of God are saying to the Body. Prophets speak fresh revelation from God which will cause strength within the Body.)

Discerning the Body of Christ

We also need to start discerning the different parts of the Body of Christ more clearly. For example, there are different anointings on different churches. Never judge one church over another, because they're all serving a purpose in the Body.

I can think of several examples in the city of Tulsa. One of my friends is a real pastor. He has a tremendous Charismatic church. Another is a teacher. He just opens his Bible and flows in that operation and administration. A third has an evangelistic church. Their emphasis is on winning souls.

We're all important to one another. We supply one another. What is tragic is when pastors don't discern the prophet's anointing; especially a prophet with a proven record. The Church *needs* the prophet's ministry to bring it light.

Pastors have invited me to their churches, saying, "I need some help. Things aren't lining up in the Spirit. Some changes need to be made, and I don't know what to do." Well, a prophet's ministry is one that deals with things in the spirit realm.

The prophet has the ability (or the grace) to speak into the spirit realm, and set a church back on course spiritually.

For example, a church may be experiencing a real attack against its finances. A prophet can go into that church, speak into the spirit realm as the Holy Spirit wills, curse that spirit of lack and poverty, and drive it off that ministry. And it works the same way with any other kind of satanic attack a church may be experiencing.

I've seen many churches turn completely around and become stronger because a prophet came in and set the spiritual atmosphere over that church in order. That prophet made diverse *deposits* into that church.

You see, this is a little-known side to a prophet. When a prophet prophesies over a church under the unction of the Holy Spirit, that church can be set on a correct course, and spiritual deposits can be made that will change that church forever.

When the prophet's anointing brings this kind of light, *believe* the prophet and obey the scriptures; you can't get around them.

When this new wave hits, we ministers are going to have to come together and help each other, accurately discerning the different parts in the Body of Christ. The ministry should not be a one-man show.

Discerning the Prophet

A man who will not listen to a prophet is not discerning the prophet's ministry, or part, that was set in the Body of Christ. Do you know what will happen to that man? He will become *weak* spiritually. He will become *sickly* in his ministry — and he could *die* prematurely! His ministry or church could also die because he didn't heed the words that a "fourstar" prophet has said.

Look at the prophet's record. You can go by the man's record, can't you? Suppose a man came to me and said, "Ed, if you will give me $1,000, I will invest it for you, and within 30 days, I'll make you $10,000." If I know the man has 50 years' experience in investments and he's hit it every time, I would listen. I would give him $1,000, and he would make me $10,000. I would look at the fruit.

You may not like what the prophet says, but look at his fruit — look at his past record. This is discerning the prophet that God put in the Body of Christ.

Just watch what will happen to pastors who disregard the prophets. All over the land you'll hear people asking,

"He had such a big church. What happened?"

"It just dwindled."

"But what happened?"

"The anointing wasn't there anymore."

"But he was such an up-and-coming young man. Oh, he could teach and preach! What happened?"

He didn't listen to what the Spirit of God said through the prophet! He said, "No, I'm not going to obey! This prophet's just *old-fashioned*, and this is a new day. He's trying to put us in bondage."

The prophet wasn't trying to put him and his church in bondage; he was bringing light on their situation. If the young pastor had listened to the illumination the prophet brought, his church would have *prospered*. As we saw earlier, that's one reason why God set the prophet in the Church.

Discerning the Pastor

God set in the Church, first apostles, then prophets, evangelists, pastors, and teachers. All of these ministries are valid. We need to discern *every one* of them.

God said *He* set pastors in the Church. That's why I'm so church-oriented. I recognize the pastor's ministry. I don't believe in people running around from church to church, or in holding renegade meetings. Some of you will always be weak in certain areas of your life if you don't discern the office of the pastor and submit to a pastor.

You ministers of the Gospel and traveling ministers, listen to me: Where's your family when you're on the road? You need to discern the pastor's ministry. Your family needs a pastor.

I know preachers whose kids act like a bunch of wild animals. When their dad is off preaching and winning the world, the kids sneak out of the house to "party" and are out riding around on motorcycles on Sunday morning when

Different Ranks and Different Anointings

they should be in church.

Verse 31 tells us we need to judge ourselves — the Church needs to judge itself — concerning the spiritual gifts that God has set in the Body of Christ. In other words, we need to discern spiritual things in the Body of Christ, and the prophet's ministry is a spiritual thing. All the gift ministries are.

I'm not taking away the importance of the ministries of the apostle, evangelist, pastor, or teacher; but the subject of this teaching is the prophet's ministry, which is very different from the other ministry gifts.

Concerning Spiritual Gifts

Now let's look at the beginning of the next chapter, First Corinthians 12:1: "Now concerning spiritual gifts, brethren, I would not have you ignorant."

I've said it in the past, and I've heard other teachers say that it should read, "Now concerning the Holy Ghost...." But that isn't true. Although Paul is talking about the Holy Ghost to a certain extent here, he's talking more about spiritual things.

Also, that word "gifts" was added by the translators of the *King James Version;* it actually isn't in the original. This verse should read, "Now concerning spiritual, brethren, I would not have you stupid or ignorant or misinformed."

Going down to the fourth verse, it says, "Now there are diversities of gifts, but the same Spirit." Notice the word "gifts" — plural. That means the gifts of the Spirit and the gift ministries that God has set in the Church.

Continuing in verses 5 and 6: "And there are differences of administrations, but the same Lord. And there are diversities of operations, but it is the same God which worketh all in all."

"Administrations" means *services, ministries,* and *offices;*

and Jesus is the Administrator. Jesus wants to be the Administrator of our services. If we allow Him to administrate, the Holy Ghost will be free to manifest Himself. He is the Manifester of what God operates and what Jesus administrates.

On the other hand, Jesus is the Prophet in the Body of Christ, and He administrates to the prophets as well as to the other ministries their services, ministries, and offices.

With that in mind, now go over to the twenty-eighth verse: "And God hath set some in the church, first apostles, secondarily prophets, thirdly teachers, after that miracles, then gifts of healings, helps, governments, diversities of tongues."

There are different types of anointings. One anointing is the mantle of a prophet — and there are different commissions for even a prophet to do, as we will now see.

Types of Prophetic Anointings

We saw in First Corinthians 12:6 that there are different *operations* and different *manifestations* in a prophet's ministry. Even as there are different *types* of prophets, they all have different *personalities*, too.

Sometimes they just act strangely. You'll be sitting talking to them — and they won't hear a word you say. Or, they'll be standing beside you, and suddenly they'll go off into the Spirit, and God will tell them something about you that will help you.

There are also different *levels* of prophets. You progress as you mature and grow. Surely God isn't going to put a strong anointing on a man who just got saved. He could have the calling of a prophet, but that doesn't mean he's going to flow under a heavy anointing right away. He first must build character and mature in other ways, just like every other believer.

Different Ranks and Different Anointings

The Rebellious Prophet

Jonah was a prophet to the world, but he must not have been too mature, for he didn't want to go to Ninevah. He said, "I'm not going there!" He took off in a ship bound in the opposite direction, and look where he ended up: in the belly of a big fish. That's right, Jonah got vomited up on the beach!

That's where a lot of preachers end up — in the belly of a big fish with a bunch of vomit — when they try to run away from their anointing! I warn you, you'll stink — you'll be in the fish's belly — if you run from God.

Actually, you will never be able to run from God, once He's called you. You will be miserable doing anything else until the day you die: You will be miserable driving a truck. You will be miserable being a salesman. You will be miserable at anything until you get up and walk in that anointing!

Men and women of God can function in different offices, but they'll be in trouble if they don't concentrate on the primary ministry God has given them.

Naturally, not every gift carries the same anointing. But whatever it is that God sanctified and ordained you to do, you've got to do. You've got to get in that groove and flow in it. If you try to do anything else, you may experience heartaches, financial problems — or even premature death, as we have just studied.

There are some television preachers who beat you over the head for finances every time they're on television. First of all, some of them are operating outside of the Word of God, because they're going around putting everyone down. This one's wrong, that one's wrong — everyone's wrong but them.

They have their own little group around them feeding them a lot of vanity. "Yes, you're right, brother. That's right. That's right. (Give me my paycheck.) That's right.

That's right." Preachers had better watch it if they have "yes" people around them feeding them vanity all the time.

I could have a big church if all I did every Sunday morning was just "hot air" everyone, if I allowed Brother and Sister Bucketmouth to do their thing, if I allowed this one to do his thing and that one to do something else, until everyone was doing whatever he wanted. I would have a crowd of people, all right, but I would also have an undisciplined, rebellious church.

The Church's Critical Hour

This is no time for rebellion! What you do in your ministry during the next two years is *crucial*. It's very important right now for *everyone* in the Body of Christ to be in the right place at the right time. Follow the leading of your spirit. This includes the prophets.

It's critical that the prophets say what the Spirit of God is saying in the next two years without backing down or worrying about being ridiculed.

What does a prophet do? He speaks for God, and that brings light into the Body of Christ. So if the prophets are not saying anything, if they're suppressed, or if they don't have the right people around them, how are they going to speak the things of God — especially when believers don't even discern their gift?

You'd *better* discern what the Spirit of God is saying through the prophets! As we saw earlier, the true prophet of God is a *seer*: He brings light to the Body of Christ when he prophesies under the unction of the Holy Ghost.

If preachers insist on being rebellious and doing their own thing, not discerning the prophet's ministry in the Body of Christ, they will pay a horrible price. They will dry up and miss the new wave in its *entirety!* The glory of God won't move in their sanctuaries, because God wants gold, not brass: He wants pure worship.

Chapter 4
Glimpses Into the Future

There are many things about the future that I want to share with you out of my spirit. God has been dealing with me about things that will happen in the Church as we come to the year 2000.

One of these things is more unity among the five-fold ministries. In the past, we've usually seen one-man shows. That's why preachers got burned out! They were trying to be jacks-of-all-trades, doing everything. If a pastor had to go out of town and he couldn't be in his pulpit one Sunday morning, he'd come under condemnation, and his people would accuse him of not doing his job.

But that isn't the way God meant for the Church to operate when He established it. He shared something with me from First Corinthians 12. Let's look at these verses.

> **And God hath set some in the church, first apostles, secondarily prophets, thirdly teachers, after that miracles, then gifts of healings, helps, governments, diversities of tongues.**
>
> **Are all apostles? . . .**
>
> **1 Corinthians 12:28, 29**

The answer to the last question is, "Of course not."

I've never shared this teaching publicly before. I've discussed it over coffee with other preachers, but I feel led in my spirit to share it with you.

The Prophet: Friend of God

Church History Will Repeat Itself

If you'll look at Church history, the Church started out with the twelve apostles of the Lamb laying the original foundation of the Church, so that foundation is complete. Today's apostles, however, build on that foundation, adding their part. Then the prophets, teachers, and others came along.

The way I'm going to bring this out is not meant to belittle the other offices whatsoever; we're all equal in the sight of God. But we all have different grace ministries. We all have different anointings, or callings, on our life.

Surely the toe doesn't have the same function as the eye, but the toe does help carry the eye around! Each of us has a different *function* in the Body of Christ.

In this century, we saw many *evangelists* come on the scene at the start of the Healing Revival in 1947. Healings, miracles, signs, and wonders were evident in their meetings.

When the Charismatic Movement swept millions of new believers into the Church in the 1960s, the Lord raised up pastors to care for them. Twenty years later, they were followed by *teachers*, who kept things on an even keel.

Now this cycle of ministries is about to end. Once it ends, it will start all over again with apostles! The Bible says the last shall be first! We're starting to hear a lot about the apostles and the prophets who are coming on the scene.

So as we come closer to the time when Jesus returns and the Church Age ends, we're going to see the restoration of the apostle's ministry. They will come to the forefront just as they did at the beginning of the Church Age.

In other words, history is going to repeat itself. It's going to do a "flip flop"! This return of the apostle's office to the Body of Christ is one of the things that lies ahead for the Church.

Glimpses Into the Future

At the present time, of course, we are seeing the emphasis shift from teachers to prophets. Their ministries complement each other.

Sometimes prophets go out in the spirit and see and say things that seem unusual. It is the job of the teachers and the other gift ministries to hear and study these spiritual matters and build a biblical foundation and teach it to the Body of Christ so the people will understand what the prophets are saying.

The Prophet's Reward Will Return

He that receiveth you receiveth me, and he that receiveth me receiveth him that sent me.

He that receiveth a prophet in the name of a prophet shall receive a prophet's reward; and he that receiveth a righteous man in the name of a righteous man shall receive a righteous man's reward.

And whosoever shall give to drink unto one of these little ones a cup of cold water only in the name of a disciple, verily I say unto you, he shall in no wise lose his reward.

Matthew 10:40-42

What does "prophet's reward" mean? The Greek word there means "to pay in wages," spiritually and in the natural. There are rewards.

Now let's go over to what I call the prophet's chapters in Second Kings. Let's talk about that reward.

People say, "I've given to prophets of God — I've given to different ministries — but I haven't gotten any reward." Let's find out why.

On a recent trip, I was ministering in a Sunday morning service, and the Lord said, "This church needs help, I want you to proclaim a reward on these people as they give in the offering this morning, for receiving you as a

The Prophet: Friend of God

prophet. I want you to proclaim a blessing over them."

As they came forward, I did what God told me to do. The results were spectacular! By the time the evening service started, people already had wonderful testimonies to give, Their financial reward in higher wages and other ways started happening to some of them that very day — in addition to the Spirit's reward they had already received.

I had never seen people so blessed, and I had never heard about this kind of financial blessing outside of Bible accounts, where you've got so much it's just overflowing, and you have to tell God to stop.

Elisha's Problem

I went back to the Bible and found some nuggets while reading about the prophets. Let's look first at Second Kings 4. Keep in mind that Elisha is president of this School of the Prophets. One of the prophets in his school died, and his widow came to see Elisha with her problem.

> **Now there cried a certain woman of the wives of the sons of the prophets unto Elisha, saying, Thy servant my husband is dead; and thou knowest that thy servant did fear the Lord: and the creditor is come to take unto him my two sons to be bondmen.**

That sounds like the present age: You must put everything you own up for collateral, almost including your kids. And if the daddy has a lot of debts, his creditors will even try to garnishee the children's paychecks to pay those debts.

Notice that the woman's husband feared the Lord.

> **And Elisha said unto her, What shall I do for thee? tell me, what hast thou in the house? And she said, Thine handmaid hath not any thing in the house, save a pot of oil.**
>
> 2 Kings 4:1, 2

Everyone, no matter how desperate he is, has *something*

in his house. And those who are not desperately poor have many things they don't use around their house — things that can be used to help finance the next great move of God!

In the coming revival, you're going to start seeing people donate their boats and everything else. Just the stuff we've got laying around our homes can support the ministry! When I said this in Florida, it didn't go over very well, because they've got big, million-dollar boats docked outside!

The Revival Will Be Funded

One afternoon after lunch, a friend and I were walking around a marina, looking at those boats, and the Lord spoke to me, saying, "All this is laid up for the just."

Wealthy people spend a million dollars for a boat and go out on it two or three times. The owners have to pay large fees to maintain and dock those expensive boats. And it's just a waste of money — a rat hole the devil uses to keep money out of the Gospel.

I said, "Boy, what a waste of money! What I could do with it! Those boats sure would buy a lot of television time!"

This is what God said to me: "I'm going to start multiplying with the working of miracles when people start giving to holy men. I want you to proclaim blessings on them when they give to your ministry. Start to teach other ministers to do the same thing so the people can be blessed." (Particularly notice that phrase "holy men.")

Elisha was a holy man. He said to the widow, "What shall I do for thee . . . what hast thou in the house?" The widow told him she had nothing "save a pot of oil." Notice what Elisha said next: "Go. . . ." Underline that word "go" in your Bible.

This story reminds me a little of blind Bartimaeus. He went after his miracle. He made a decision that he was going to get it; it didn't matter what anyone said about him.

The Prophet: Friend of God

They told him to shut up, but he kept going after it. He wasn't going to shut up.

We, too, are going to have to start using our faith. We give up too easily. We get discouraged too easily. *We need to fight for what belongs to us!*

Faith will always go toward the miracle! We see this in John 11, where Jesus kept telling His disciples, "Let's go. Let's go toward the miracle." They were going toward Bethany, where Jesus' friend Lazarus was already in his grave.

Obey the Word of God. Then go toward the miracle you seek, acting like you've already got it. Speak words of faith about your problem as if you've got the answer, even if it hasn't manifested yet. When you pray, believe that you receive. Believe you've got the answer right now. It's already yours, it's settled!

"Well, it doesn't *look* like it, Brother Ed."

You're going by the natural senses, but I'm going by what the Word says. If the Word says I'm healed, then I'm healed. If the Word says my needs are taken care of, then they're taken care of. I don't care what the devil and all his cohorts (and all their friends in the natural) say. I'm going toward my miracle, glory to God!

Elisha didn't tell the widow what he was going to do to bring about her miracle. All he said was, "Go, borrow thee vessels abroad of all thy neighbours, even empty vessels; borrow not a few" (v. 3).

Will You Limit the Size of Your Blessing?

That sounds like she's the one who's going to limit this blessing! Her miracle will be limited by the number of containers she brings. (I'd get every vessel in town if a prophet told me, "Go get them, because they're going to be filled up.")

Then he told her, "And when thou art come in, thou shalt shut the door upon thee and upon thy sons, and shalt pour out into all those vessels, and thou shalt set aside that which is full" (v. 4).

Notice she obeyed the man of God: "So she went from him, and shut the door upon her and upon her sons, who brought the vessels to her, and she poured out" (v. 5). She poured out. You know, you're going to have to obey the Word and give out. Hoarded things aren't going to get you the blessings you want.

"And it came to pass, when the vessels were full, that she said unto her son, Bring me yet a vessel. And he said unto her, There is not a vessel more. And the oil stayed" (v. 6).

That means it stopped flowing. Some people get money, such as an inheritance, and they blow it. It flows right through their fingers. It runs out.

Sad to say, most Christians don't know how to handle their money at all. They don't tithe to God; they don't help the poor; they don't do what God ways. They try to excuse themselves by saying, "Well, I'm so far in debt, I can't tithe anything."

Start where you're at. Start tithing to God and see what happens. He said in His Word that He changes not. He's the same yesterday, today, and forever.

Then she came and told the man of God. And he said, Go, sell the oil, and pay thy debt, and live thou and thy children of the rest" (v. 7). Underline this word "go."

How many of you would like to pay your creditors? I like to pay mine. This widow had so much money left, she lived the rest of her life on it!

Financial Miracles Will Come!

From the things that are in my spirit, I believe we're going to see similar miracles happen in the future. There's not much time left before the Lord returns. It's going to take a lot of finances to get the job of evangelization done, so we're going to need some working of financial miracles

The Prophet: Friend of God

in our lives.

We're going to see some men of God do strange things. One may ask you for your last dime, like Elisha asked the widow. Only this time it won't be a gimmick, as we've seen in the past. (Nevertheless, you must prayerfully discern all such requests.)

Continuing in this fourth chapter of Second Kings, we see Elisha encounter another woman of faith.

"And it fell on a day, that Elisha passed to Shunem, where was a great woman; and she constrained him to eat bread. And so it was, that as oft as he passed by, he turned in thither to eat bread" (v. 8). This was a well-known woman, a wealthy woman, who persuaded the prophet to honor her home with his presence.

'I Perceive That This Is An Holy Man'

"And she said unto her husband, Behold now, I perceive that this is *an holy man* of God, which passeth by us continually" (v. 9). That phrase "holy man" jumped out at me. Underline it. I said to myself, "I wonder how many people think I'm a holy man?" Have you preachers ever wondered that about yourself?

Too many Christians, including Bible school students, have a bad credit rating. We live like the world. We lie like the world. That's why sinners laugh at us: We don't live godly lives because of the simple fact that we've got the world in us.

The phone rings, and your wife says, "He isn't home right now" — and you're sitting right there in the front room. Before you know it, you've seared your conscience to the point that you don't tell the truth anymore, and you don't even realize that you're no longer a *holy* man of God. You're a *sinner*.

God told me while I was in Florida, "The reason why a lot of people aren't getting returns and being blessed is

Glimpses Into the Future

because they're not giving to *holy men.*"

This great woman in Shunem *perceived* that Elisha was *a holy man,* and she asked her husband, "Let us make a little chamber, I pray thee, on the wall; and let us set for him there a bed, and a table, and a stool, and a candlestick: and it shall be when he cometh to us, that he shall turn in thither" (v. 10).

Some teach that this prophet's chamber was actually in the front of the house, over the porch. They believe it was a beautiful room of considerable size, and it was furnished handsomely. In fact, they think the "stool" was really a throne built especially for the prophet.

"We've got a prophet's quarters," pastors have boasted to me. I've stayed in those prophet's quarters. They're furnished with used furniture dating from 1942. The bed is rickety and everything else is beat up, too.

Faithfulness Will Be Rewarded

Now we're coming to the part with the nuggets:

> And it fell on a day, that he [Elisha] came thither, and he turned into the chamber, and lay there.
>
> And he said to Gehazi his servant, Call this Shunammite. And when he had called her, she stood before him.
>
> And he said unto him, Say now unto her, Behold, *thou hast been careful for us* with all this care; *what is to be done for thee?* wouldest thou be spoken for to the king, or to the captain of the host? And she answered, I dwell among mine own people.
>
> 2 Kings 4:11-13

Here's another word to underline: "careful." Those words "careful" and "care" jumped off the page when I was meditating on that passage one day. Elisha was saying, "You were very careful to take care of us."

God told me we have not been very careful to take care of the men of God in our day. I want you to know this, my brother and sister: When you don't take care of the men of God, you're not taking care of Jesus.

You've got to realize that the fivefold ministry is not a gift of the Holy Spirit, it's a gift from Jesus, the Head of the Church. It's a gift output of Jesus' ministry. So we must be careful to take care of the men of God.

Some churches that haven't done this properly are deep in debt, even to the point of just paying the interest on their loans. You see, when spiritual leaders are not treated properly by churches or other ministries, it will always take a toll on them and their ministry.

"What Do You Need?"

The return to the great woman of Shunem came when Elisha asked her, "What is to be done for thee?" Oh, I like that! I'd never done that until God told me, "When people bless you and take care of you, I want you to start asking them, 'Pastor, what do you need in this church? Do you need a new addition to your building?' "

You'd be surprised how many pastors fight me concerning airfare and everything else when they invite me to come preach in their church! They want me to pay for everything, including my wife's airfare, and then take all of *their* expenses out of *my* love offering. That isn't being careful.

You know, if you can't take care of a man of God, don't invite him. I'm tired of all this jiving: "Oh, brother, we love you, but. . . ." I'm just telling you why people aren't getting blessed! Ministers are going to have to start being honest in their dealings with others.

When I want to hold a special meeting like our Fresh Oil Conference, I count the cost first, and then I start putting a little money aside. That way we can take care of our speakers properly, without having to dip into their love offering to pay bills. There's a reward in wages that comes with the prophet's ministry when you bless them and take care of them.

That's why Elisha asked the woman, "What can I do for thee?" He's a prophet of God. The prophets are not only *coming;* they are already here. They're getting set up all over the world. You're going to see the prophets and the apostles in full power in the last days before Jesus comes.

A New Look at the Gift Ministries

I'm getting my thinking on the gift ministries changed around. God's dealing with this boy, too. We've always thought that the pastor had the principal ministry, and the rest were nothing but stepchildren who were allowed to come to church and beg for finances, although they actually have a part of the tithe anyway!

The pastor has always been on the scene controlling all the tithes in the local church. That's why all the other ministries had to go out as stepchildren and have mailing lists and everything else. But that isn't the way God established it.

The tithe should be for all the workers in the Body of Christ who are functioning. The tithe is for the workers; not to build buildings. That's the way it should be.

The way it's been is that the rest of the ministry gifts have always had to beg. "Be careful," we've been told. "Don't get the pastor upset. If you say anything about money, he'll get upset." Well, it's not his money to begin with. It's God's money, and it needs to go to all the workers. The pastor is not the only worker in the Body of Christ. There are four other ministry gifts that do the work of God as well.

We've got to stop all that junk. We've got to get it *right.* (I'd love to share this at a pastors' convention!) It amazes me that they'll ask a pastor to talk at a pastors' convention

The Prophet: Friend of God

about the traveling ministry when he's never done any traveling.

There is so much disrespect for men of God today. Everyone laughs at those who have fallen — even the Christians are laughing. When preachers start talking about their money and calling them crooks, it grieves me. It's nothing but a trick of the devil. I tell them, "Excuse me, I'm going to my room. I'm not going to let my ears fill up with that junk about any other preacher."

Some preachers are so afraid of the media talking about the prosperity of Christians that they're selling their homes and buying little cracker box houses. We're going to have to get rid of this fear of men. (I'm not talking about squandering money.) We've got to get back to where there is a respect for holy men of God.

The reason many of you haven't been getting blessed is because you haven't been giving to *holy* men of God. You've been giving because people put emotional pressure on you through the mail or other means.

Prophets Will Get Results

The careful woman is about to get her reward. "Wouldest thou be spoken for to the king, or to the captain of the host?" She answered the servant, "I dwell among mine own people." She meant, "I've already got social status." She was a wealthy woman. It took a lot of money to build that addition onto her house.

The prophet asked his servant further, "What then is to be done for her? and Gehazi answered, Verily she hath no child, and her husband is old" (v. 14).

"And he said, Call her. And when he had called her, she stood in the door. And he [the prophet] said. . . ." This is what the Lord has been dealing with me about. This is what prophets — holy men — are going to say, *When they speak, they are going to get results!*

Elisha told the woman, ". . . About this season, according to the time of life, thou shalt embrace a son. And she said, Nay, my lord, thou man of God, do not lie unto thine handmaid" (v. 16).

This is happening a great deal today, too. Prophecies are being given, but people don't believe them. Of course, we've had a lot of goofies going around prophesying all kinds of things.

The Miracle Came!

"About this season, according to the time of life, thou shalt embrace a son. . . ." You might as well get ready; you're going to have a son, great woman! "And the woman conceived, and bare a son at that season that Elisha had said unto her, according to the time of life." God performed a miracle for this barren couple.

Fifteen to eighteen years passed between this verse and the next, for the story that is building in this chapter leaps ahead to when the boy is grown.

"And when the child was grown, it fell on a day, that he went out to his father to the reapers. And he said unto his father, My head, my head. And he said to a lad, Carry him to his mother. And when he had taken him, and brought him to his mother, he sat on her knees till noon, and then died" (vv. 18-20).

He died.

It looked like the prophet of God missed it.

In the good times, we gain a lot of knowledge out of the Word of God. Yet when bad things happen, we drop out — we don't stay hooked up to the Word.

For example, if you start having financial problems, you'll be tempted to say, "Well, tithing doesn't work," and if you're not careful, you'll stop tithing.

The Word is always true. Just stay with it, and that situation in your life will change. The Word will never change, so the situation has to. The Word is the same yesterday, today, and forever. And that's the way we ought to be in our walk with God.

Fight for Your Miracle

If a man of God gives you a prophecy, and if he's a holy man of God, then stand on that word until it defeats the devil. Those blessings are going to come on you. But you're going to have to fight the devil for them, because he wants to steal that word, that prophecy, from you. He will try to steal your health, too. Fight the devil. Don't fight people; fight the devil for what belongs to you.

Healing belongs to you. Fight for it. Prosperity belongs to you. Fight for it! It's God's will for you. So don't listen to a bunch of ungodly people who are laughing about preachers who fell, and don't read ungodly books written by so-called Christians who would talk you out of faith.

I refuse this junk anymore! I'm taking a stronger and stronger stand on the Word of God. I was very strong about it when I got born again in 1970. I really got turned onto the Word.

But in the last few years, I've gotten to be kind of a pantywaist on it, or I'd find it easier to take a pill than believe God for my healing.

Some would say, "There are different healing flows of the Spirit." No, there's only *one* flow, and that's from God. And, bless God, it belongs to us!

We don't fight hard enough. We don't get in the Word of God and fight for what belongs to us! Then we get flaky. We do weird things financially. We do weird things with our bodies and everything else. We need to get in line with the Word of God and do what it says!

A Test of Great Faith

The woman's son died. "And she went up, and laid him on the bed of the man of God, and shut the door upon him, and went out" (v. 21).

I want you to look at this woman's faith. She knew about the prophet's ministry. It was a little different in those days. (It's even stronger today.)

In those days, people went to the prophet of God for guidance all the time. Actually, the prophet of God controlled the people, because that was the only way they could get guidance from God for their life. Today we have the Holy Spirit within us, giving us guidance. But why not have the same kind of faith this great woman had? If we did, we'd get the results she got!

She knew about the anointing that was on the prophet's mantle! She placed her dead son's body on the prophet's bed, walked out, and shut the door.

"And she called unto her husband, and said, Send me, I pray thee, one of the young men, and one of the asses, that I may run to the man of God, and come again. And he said, Wherefore wilt thou go to him to day? it is neither new moon, nor sabbath. And she said, *It shall be well*" (vv. 22, 23).

Her husband said, "Why are you going to see the prophet? It isn't time for church. What are you talking about?"

And she said, "It will be all right."

She didn't even tell him their son was dead.

Concentrating on the Results

Faith people who believe in the end results don't blab about all the problems they're having. This woman knew what the end results were going to be. I like this woman's faith. She had the God-kind of faith, not the flaky-kind

The Prophet: Friend of God

of faith!

She reminds me of the woman with the issue of blood, who said, "If I may but touch his garment, I shall be healed." She locked in. The Shunammite also reminds me of blind Bartimaeus. He locked into faith and got his miracle, too.

How many of you want results in your life? I'm tired of playing religion. I'm tired of these games people play. You can't ride the fence.

We're going to have to believe what the Word of God says. We're going to have to get back to the Bible for our finances, healing, and every other area of life, walking holy before God.

Better Returns on Your Giving

God said the people are going to have to start giving to holy men, and they will get better results on their finances. They're going to have to check ministries out and see if the leaders are holy men of God or not.

"Then she saddled an ass, and said to her servant, Drive, and go forward; slack not thy riding for me, except I bid thee" (v. 24).

She got into her Cadillac. Not everyone was wealthy enough to own a donkey in those days. She and the servant *moved!* This woman was in a hurry.

"So she went and came unto the man of God to Mount Carmel. And it came to pass, when the man of God saw her afar off, that he said to Gehazi his servant, Behold, yonder is that Shunammite: Run now, I pray thee, to meet her, and say unto her, Is it well with thee? is it well with thy husband? is it well with the child? And she answered, It is well" (vv. 25-26).

She didn't talk about her problem. She said, "It is well." Quit talking about your problems. You can deal with them. The trouble with Christians is, they get into the natural and they don't want to deal with problems. They say it's faith when it's stupidity. A problem is a problem.

Dealing With Reality

A fellow we know needs a new liver. That's a problem. That's something you have to deal with. That is the truth. But there is a higher truth that says that God will meet all of our needs according to His riches in glory.

You have to deal with it. You can't say, "Well, that problem really isn't there." No, that's getting into Christian Science. We don't deny reality; we deal with it. How do we deal with it? *With the Word of God!*

Some of you have a problem: You need to get your finances straightened out. Start paying your tithes. Start dealing with your problems and see what God will do for you. And quit saying, "Well, God will take care of all my needs" while bill collectors are calling you. No, you have to deal with those problems.

"It is well with me."

"And when she came to the man of God to the hill, she caught him by the feet, but Gehazi came near to thrust her away. And the man of God said, Let her alone; for her soul is vexed within her: and the Lord hath hid it from me, and hath not told me" (v. 27).

She didn't mess around! She caught the prophet by the feet. Gehazi tried to push her away (that's the ministry of helps). Notice that the prophet didn't know about her problem. Prophets don't know everything. Elisha said, "It's hidden from me. I don't know what her problem is."

"Then she said, Did I desire a son of my lord? did I not say, Do not deceive me?" (v. 28).

I like the faith of this woman. Most people would have quit then.

The Importance of Standing in Faith

She said, "You're a prophet of God. And I got my pay in wages. But that pay didn't last. My child died. Now, don't you deceive me. Don't you lie to me!"

"Then he said to Gehazi, Gird up thy loins, and take my staff in thine hand and go thy way: if thou meet any man, salute him not, and if any salute thee, answer him not again: and lay my staff upon the face of the child" (v. 29).

Sometimes the staff isn't good enough.

"And the mother of the child said, As the Lord liveth, and as thy soul liveth, I will not leave thee. . . ."

There's something about making up your mind to stand in faith until hell freezes over that makes God move on your behalf. Brother Smith Wigglesworth said, "You make the decision that you're going to stand in faith, and God will go over a million people just to get to you." God honors faith!

"And he [Elisha] arose and followed her" (v. 30). I guess so!

"And Gehazi passed on before them, and laid the staff upon the face of the child; but there was neither voice, nor hearing. Wherefore he went again to meet him, and told him, saying, The child is not awaked.

"And when Elisha was come into the house, behold, the child was dead, and laid upon his bed.

"He went in therefore, and shut the door upon them twain, and prayed unto the Lord" (vv. 31-33).

No Fast-Food Prayer Life

A lot of us give up because we don't get instant results. We get in a hurry. Instead of praying, "How do You want me to do this, Lord?" We say, "Well, I guess it isn't God's will to heal."

Glimpses Into the Future

I want you to see that the man of God went into that room to get results. He prayed.

People are different, and there are different ways to deal with them. Study the ministries of Jesus, John Alexander Dowie, Maria Woodworth-Etter, Smith Wigglesworth, John G. Lake, and others. They dealt with people differently.

Jesus spit on people. Sometimes He'd make mud and put it in their eyes.

But our generation of instant-everything is in a hurry. We enter a sick room and expect instant results. Just because we eat at fast-food restaurants doesn't mean we can do that with our prayer life.

There are times when you're going to have to get before God and pray for long seasons, even though it would be easier to lay your flesh down on the couch and turn the television set on, saying, "Well, in the Name of Jesus, I believe that I receive it. Amen."

"And he went up, and lay upon the child, and put his mouth upon his mouth, and his eyes upon his eyes, and his hands upon his hands: and he stretched himself upon the child; and the flesh of the child waxed warm.

"Then he returned, and walked in the house to and fro; and went up, and stretched himself upon him: and the child sneezed seven times, and the child opened his eyes" (vv. 34, 35).

I want you to know that this woman got her prophet's pay in wages right then, about eighteen years later.

Claim Your Prophet's Reward

God told me that there will be a time when people are going to need a miracle, and if you have taken care of a man of God, you've got a prophet's reward coming. You can stand in faith and get it. You have a right to it. I know there have been lots of gimmicks used to squeeze money out of believers, but this isn't a gimmick. This is the Word of God.

The great woman got her return. She got her pay in wages. She got her child raised from the dead! Years after taking care of a prophet, her prophet's reward still worked.

Praise God, we're going to see the prophet's ministry come on the scene. It doesn't do away with the other gift ministries; it adds to them.

Some of you need your finances raised from the dead. Some of you need your bodies raised from the death bed. God has provided a way for each one of us to get our needs met.

The Coming Wave of Healing

One of the things God has told me about the future concerns a mighty wave of healing. He said, "A day is coming in the nineties when there is going to be such a revival of healing that hospitals are going to be emptied out by the power of God."

He continued, "People are going to come to churches where that healing power is flowing. People are going to be set free, and it's going to hurt the medical profession so much that lawsuits will start coming against the church from that industry." (They'll claim we are practicing medicine without a license.)

If you are involved in the field of medicine, or if you're a doctor, please don't get touchy and say I'm against doctors. I am *not* against doctors! Praise God for doctors. Praise God for hospitals. They are not the ones who heal, but God will use doctors to heal you. What I'm saying is that Jesus is the Healer.

Also, the Lord showed me that's one reason why we're going to need a satellite dish on our property in the nineties. We'll need access to satellites, because commercial networks won't allow healing ministries on television in the nineties. No matter what price they're offered, they won't allow programs with healing to be on the air.

They don't even know the True Church is alive yet. They know nothing about us — but wait till we get going!

The Healing Waters Will Flow

In talking to different television engineers, I learned that in the near future, tiny satellite dishes will be available that you can put on top of your TV set, and you'll be able to pick up everything off the satellites. That's what we'll need. In the nineties, we want to shoot our services up to a satellite so people can pick them up.

Can't you just picture a big guy sitting in his living room eating a submarine sandwich and holding a can of beer? All of a sudden he flips across the dial and the anointing hits him, knocks that beer can out of his hand — and straightens his baby's leg in the Name of Jesus. He'll get saved right there, glory to God!

So I'm getting in position for the 1990's to be ready when the next wave hits. It's coming! It's starting to happen now — a little bit here and a little bit there. It's going to get stronger and stronger.

My brother and sister, it is vital that all of us be in the right position; especially in the next two years. If you're anchored down and ready to go, you'll be able to flow with it.

That's why we wrote the book *Fresh Oil From Heaven* — to get this message out into the Body of Christ for people to get into position.

Prosper Through the Prophet's Anointing

Are you listening to me, Church? What is the Spirit of God saying to the prophets? Listen to what they are saying, and you'll have insight into what is about to happen.

When the prophets say good times are coming in the economy, it's the time to buy and sell. But when they say,

The Prophet: Friend of God

"Don't get into debt," pull back and you will make it through that period. The prophet's anointing brings light, and when you obey, you'll prosper!

Of course, there are some secrets that prophets can't speak out yet. The Lord can't reveal these secrets to baby prophets who are being incubated and trained now.

It's good for these young prophets to work for a while around a prophet who has matured under that anointing. They will learn the things of the Spirit, as Elisha learned from Elijah, and they will then be able to flow in the Spirit.

There are more prophets around than you think. They're all over this land. In fact, there are prophets who are placed over cities and nations. That's why we need to pray for the prophets to come forth. And they are! The prophets are coming! (One reason is because teachers planted the seed of the prophet's ministry.)

The gift ministries' job is to equip the saints, so if you don't know what you're supposed to do in the Body of Christ, let the pastor, the evangelist, the teacher, the prophet, and the apostle help guide and equip you.

Creating an Atmosphere for Miracles

Some are arguing about the Trinity. How is that going to equip you to help people? When people ask me, "Which way do you believe?" I say, "I don't have a position on that. I don't have time to fuss and fight about where the Spirit is. I just want Him to work."

I don't care *how* spiritual power works, but I do want it to work like an automobile. I'm not too concerned with how an automobile runs. I want to know how to put the key into the ignition and get it started, go where I need to go, and get that person healed or delivered.

That's why I don't need to find out where God came from. (Honey, your brain couldn't handle it if you *did* know

Glimpses Into the Future

where He came from! You would blow a fuse!)

But people have many questions. Someone asked me, "Well, how does tongues work?"

I replied, "Some of it I don't understand with my natural mind. I don't always know what I'm saying in tongues when I get in the Spirit. Yet it works. It works."

They say, "I've watched you. Why do you jerk?"

"I don't know," I tell them. "When the anointing hits me, I jerk."

"Well, where does it come from?"

"Just as long as it gets someone healed, I don't care. I just know it comes from heaven."

If I could stand on my head and get someone healed, I'd stand on my head. I don't care. If I ran around the auditorium seven times and everyone fell under the power and got a vision of their ministry, I'd do it — whatever it would take. I wouldn't ask any questions — I'd just do it! A true servant doesn't ask any questions, he just obeys the words of his master.

Obedience always creates an atmosphere for miracles. We saw that with the Shunammite woman. You young prophets need to heed this advice. Don't try to figure everything out in your head. Just obey the voice of the Lord!

The Prophet's People

I don't know why, but *the devil hates prophets!* He will try to destroy their family. He will try to destroy a prophet any way he can. That's why it's important for a prophet to have the right people around him.

When you have been around a prophet's ministry, you learn to recognize that deeper anointing, and you learn when it's about to begin operating. You also learn what kind of music (especially from the minstrel) and what kind of ministry it takes to pull on the prophet's mantle.

The Prophet: Friend of God

Thus, it's important that prophets have people around them who understand the prophet's ministry and who can help the prophet yield to his anointing.

For a complete list of tapes and books by
Ed Dufresne, and to be on his mailing list,
please write:

Ed Dufresne Ministries
P.O. Box 186
Temecula, CA 92593